WHY  HATE THE POOR?

Published by Diviacchi Promotions, Inc.
Boston, MA. 2021

Table of Contents

Lilies of the Field

Why are you anxious about clothing?
Consider the lilies of the field, how they grow.
They don't toil, neither do they spin.

So says the bible. This saying along with the Parable of the Workers in the Vineyard (which I will contemplate in a later essay) long ago convinced me that God hates the poor.

Before and during the Big Dig Project in Boston, there were two lilies in particular I remember. One was this old, twisted, dirty, broken, pear tree growing in some broken up gravel in a parking lot crevice between a fence and a concrete support left over from something but I never knew what. The other was some kind of yellow flower growing in a crack in the construction barriers between the northbound and southbound lanes of Interstate 93 that was an elevated highway at that time.

The pear tree had been growing in that same spot for so long that part of the parking lot fence was encased in its bark. It never grew to more than six or seven feet tall. Its bark was wrinkled with cuts and ridges, there was no smooth part anywhere on it. It probably tried to grow higher but could never make it, someone or something would always wind up breaking any branch that got too far from the trunk. I watched it for about four to five years come to life every Spring, put out skinny green leaves, and then some sad excuses for white blossoms. At some point in late Summer, it then put out a small handful of the smallest yellow and black pears that I had ever seen. I had no idea how long it had been growing there. Given the fence encased in its bark, it must have been quite awhile. No one watered it, no one fertilized it, no one took care of it, and no one cared for it. Most definitely, no one talked to it and it never had a companion. Yet, regardless of Summer heat, Winter cold, flood, or drought, it lived. Almost every workday I saw it as I walked by; it seem to me to be one of the most beautiful of lilies. One night, the Big Dig decided to rip up the parking lot. Next day, I went to work and it was gone. Gone without a trace, as if it never existed. There will be no elegy in any churchyard to mourn its passing.

In crossing over Interstate 93 via a walkway that existed at one time, one year in the Spring I saw this big yellow flower growing in a crack next to one of the highway's north-south lane barriers. Traffic on one side was traveling six inches to a foot away 24/7 at 65 mph on average during non rush hour. During rush-hour, I would guess thousands of cars crawled by it every hour. It was a big bright flower, I could see it clearly a good 50 – 60 feet away, but I never knew what kind it was. No one watered it, no one fertilized it, no one took care of it, and no one cared for it. Yet, regardless of the Summer heat and the Summer drought of that year in which it barely rained in July and August, it lived growing in concrete. Every workday I saw it live its solitary life either from my office window or walking by on the walkway; it also seem to me to be one of the most beautiful of lilies of that Summer. One night in late Summer, the Big Dig closed that section of highway and ripped up the barriers during the night. Next morning, I went to work and it was gone without a trace, as if it never existed. There will be no elegy in any churchyard to mourn its passing.

This is how God takes care of his lilies of the field. More accurately, this is how His lilies take care of themselves in spite of having Him as caretaker.

In the area where my beloved pear tree and highway flower once grew, there now are some gardens of the Rose Fitzgerald Kennedy Greenway maintained by the Rose Fitzgerald Kennedy Greenway Conservancy. These Greenway gardens contain a wide variety of all types of flowers, including so-called "wild flowers", in carefully manicured plots that are well maintained, well watered (usually with a sprinkler system), well fertilized, and above all maintained by design in an organic and "natural state". Humanity's "lilies of the field" consisting of idle rich Boston philanthropists and their chosen government agents, artists, and humanists who make up the Conservancy would not allow their wage workers to maintain their gardens in any other way. Often, the Conservancy has meetings in the gardens in which they discuss the beauty of the world they have created in their image to which they invite visiting "artists" whose "art" is a further topic of discussion. One year, artist Janet Echelman at a six-figure cost hung a big multicolored net between buildings above a portion of the Greenway gardens so that the Conservancy's gods and lilies of the field could look up at it and experience the beauty of her art as if it were a sail moving in the wind — like the sails moving around for free in Boston Harbor just a couple of hundred feet away.

2

The purpose of this expensive art was so that these gods and their lilies of the field while in their gardens could look up to their heaven and feel how exceptional they were for being able to appreciate such art instead of thinking it to be a complete waste of their trust fund money and of tax dollars as most *hoi polloi* would think.

Well, they can all go fuck themselves. Individually or in combination, the pear tree and highway flower in their struggles for life whether in concrete or in the farce called the natural world were more beautiful and have given me a collection of more beautiful and inspiring memories that are a further basis for both philosophical and pragmatic thought than anything the Conservancy, its demigods or lilies of the fields, or their self-centered delusion called art have ever done or will do.

On this presidential inauguration date, a few will celebrate their notoriety in history gained at the expense of millions of forever unknown souls. Most workers once they have had some time to contemplate after work celebrate only "meet the new boss same as the old boss" instead of being followers who cry for or worship their old or new leaders. In memory of my parking lot pear tree and my highway yellow flower and the billions of God-made not demigod-made lilies of the field who have made this world and hopefully will make the future once they renew their will to power and fight the powers-that-be, I publish one of the few citations from a President's inauguration speech that are worth knowing and repeating:

It is not the critic who counts; not the man who points out how the strong man stumbles, or where the doer of deeds could have done them better. The credit belongs to the man who is actually in the arena, whose face is marred by dust and sweat and blood; who strives valiantly; who errs, who comes short again and again, because there is no effort without error and shortcoming; but who does actually strive to do the deeds; who knows great enthusiasms, the great devotions; who spends himself in a worthy cause; who at the best knows in the end the triumph of high achievement, and who at the worst, if he fails, at least fails while daring greatly, so that his place shall never be with those cold and timid souls who neither know victory nor defeat. --- Theodore Roosevelt (Inauguration speech)

Why Does God Hate the Poor? Prologue / Part I

Why does God hate the poor? This is a question that is very difficult to analyze rationally because of the nature of reason. Other than for logical techniques such as mathematics and pure logic, reason seems only to be capable of expressing pragmatic truth about the subject matter of its reasoning. That is, it only serves as a tool for solving a given problem and that solution can only be proven false by the problem — when the solution fails. Reason can never provide solutions that are true in all possible worlds nor can it state a truth that is true in all possible worlds. I say "seems" because when reason expresses doubt about its ability for certainty, it disproves its own skepticism either by formally stating that it is true there is no truth or by stating it is absolutely true that all truth is contingent or relative. Using "seems" to try to get around or to describe this problem or limitation of human reason causes its own problems.

What does "seems" mean? Does rational thought necessarily lead to a phenomenological view of reality that is worthless for anything but allowing academics to generate endless verbiage saying nothing about "nothing" — since according to them there's nothing except what they are saying about the nothing that is out there for which we need them to "deconstruct" it for us. If I do not know what is out there, how can it "seem" like something or anything? What does "seem" mean? What does any word mean? These are problems in the philosophy of language that are beyond the limitations of these essays. We just need to be aware of these problems when we try to contemplate questions such as this dealing with the nature of God.

I am trying to deal here with a real problem that has troubled many philosophers and myself my whole life: why does God hate the poor? Trying to resolve this problem in any way through religious faith, especially by Christian faith, always fails me; so this problem continues to bother me. Responding to this problem by telling me that life is not a problem to be solved but a mystery or reality to be experienced only makes it worse by proving the severity of the problem. Why are there some people in life who have enough time on their hands and the opportunity not only to sit around and abstractly come up with bullshit such as this, but they also have the motive, opportunity, and ability then to go around and if not lecture at least to profess to others that life should be a mystery or what life should be while the majority of the world, including me, is simply trying to survive and are responding on a daily basis to problems and situations trying to destroy that survival. Sure, telling the poor that they should be poor in spirit as well as poor materially would solve their spiritual suffering, if not their physical suffering, but why should anyone be poor in spirit and poor in material wealth and poor in their options in life when it is just as possible to be wealthy and powerful and to be poor in spirit?

The so-called Church Father St. Augustine is a perfect example to what I am referring. He spends most of his life wealthy, carousing, fornicating, fathering and abandoning children, drinking, and generally having an overall great time, until he gets bored with such worldly pleasures and decides that he wants to possess outer- worldly pleasures. So, he decides to be saved by belief in Jesus Christ. And now with the certainty of eternal life in Heaven, he goes around lecturing to others to be poor and not to live life carousing, fornicating, fathering and abandoning children, drinking, and generally having an overall great time. Even with this conversion, he does not become poor in spirit or materially in any way. Instead of being a Power-that-be among the upper class of his native city of Hippo in North Africa, he becomes a Power-that-be among the new Power in antiquity, the Christian Church. It was perfect timing. If he had stayed a rich pagan, his class might have expected him to risk his life and to defend the city against the barbarian Vandals coming to destroy them. "Barbarian" is a word to describe ambitious poor people that are trying to become rich. Instead, by converting and becoming a church father, he avoided this personal and economic risk because the Vandals respected the Church, Church property, and its ministers. The rich always get away with such hypocrisy. President George W. Bush is a great modern example. Here is a dude that spends most of his life as a lazy, ignorant, cokehead; who wastes what little education his family paid for him to receive and wastes all the business opportunities he had; until one day he decides he wants to be president of the United States. At that point, he sees the light of Christianity and goes on to use preaching and his family connections to become President and start two wars in which others do his killing for him.

I'm fully aware that by making such complaints I come off as greedy, whiny, and spiteful, as the poor usually do when complaining about their lot in life — unless they reach the point of complete depression, desperation, or starving in the street, at which point they become a temporary object of pity and charity for the rich. If the poor materially try to fight their way out of hopelessness and material poverty, they are considered greedy and spiteful barbarians again. Unlike the rich and powerful whose greed, ambition, and aggressive competitiveness are the forces that move the economic world throughout history to be sustainable and evolve, regardless of whether you call it barter, mercantilism, imperialism, capitalism, or whatever the present day economic "-ism" may be. My intent here is not to complain about this as a problem. Such would be a waste and equivalent to complaining about it becoming dark at night. It is an undisputed and unchanging fact of life that cannot be altered by human action that humanity

6

is and always will be divided into the powerful who can create meaning in life and the remainder of the powerless whose meaning in life is to serve the meaning created by the powerful with their only other choice being a lifetime of struggle, fight, and battle against that meaning — a meaningless struggle that they will always be destined to lose. The details of this division in human nature were best described by George Orwell in his book 1984 which I will contemplate.

For any amateur Christian theologians out there who may read this, I want to point out that this issue is also a Christian theological issue. The New Testament quotes Jesus several times as saying, "The poor, you will always have with you." — Matthew 26:11, Mark 14:7, and John 12:8. So this is not only a philosophical issue, but also a significant theological issue.

Why Does God Hate the Poor? Prologue / Part II

Why does God hate the poor? It is not my intent to complain about this problem. Such would be a waste and equivalent to complaining about it becoming dark at night. I accept as an indisputable and unchanging fact of life that cannot be altered by human action that humanity always will be as George Orwell described it; I quote him from his book <u>1984</u>:

> *Throughout recorded time and probably since the end of the Neolithic Age, there have been three kinds of people in the world. The high, the middle, and the low. They have been subdivided in many ways, they've born countless different names, and their relative numbers, as well as their attitude toward one another, have varied from age to age. But the essential structure of society is never altered. Even after enormous upheavals and seemingly irrevocable changes, the same pattern has always reasserted itself. Just as a gyroscope will always return to equilibrium however far it's pushed one way or the other. The aims of these three groups are entirely irreconcilable. The aim of the high is to remain where they are. The aim of the middle is to change places with the high. The aim of the low, where they to have any aim, for it is an abiding characteristic of the low that they are too much crushed by drudgery, to be more than intermittently conscious of anything outside their daily lives, is to abolish all distinctions and create a society in which all men shall be equal. Thus throughout history's struggle, which is the same in its main outlines, reoccurs over and over again. For long periods, the high seem to be securely in power, but sooner or later there always comes a moment when they lose either their belief in themselves, or their capacity to govern efficiently, or both. They are then overthrown by the middle, who enlist the low on their side by pretending to them that they are fighting for liberty and justice. As soon as they have reached their objective, the middle thrusts the low back into their old position of servitude, and themselves become the high. Presently a new middle group splits off from one of the other groups, or from both of them, and the struggle begins over again. Of the three groups, only the low are never even temporarily successful in achieving their aims.*

> *Would it be an exaggeration to say that throughout history, there has been no progress of any material kind? Even today, in a period of decline, the average human being is physically better off than he was a few centuries ago, but no advance in wealth, no*

*softening of manners, no reform or revolution has ever brought
humanity, human equality, any millimeter nearer. From the point of
view of the low, no historical change has ever meant much more
than a change in the name of their masters.*

The only problem with this great description of reality by George
Orwell is its limitation to recorded time. Even assuming there is such a thing
as unrecorded time as distinct from recorded time, separation of humans into
the lows and highs seems not to be limited to any social construct but seems
to be an undisputed absolute truth of human nature. In all possible worlds in
which there are human beings, this social construct will exist and thus it is
not solely a social construct. All humans living and treating each other as
equals and loving each other may be a vision of Heaven but would be a
short, boring, mind-numbing, lazy, life on earth. Without struggle and battle
for something, human life would be shallow, boring, cowardly, and short —
unless you were self-centered enough to become an amoral god ignoring
reality to live in the timeliness and thus the power of the moment throughout
a shallow, cowardly, and passionless life.

Phrasing the problem as a matter of evil existing in the world
misstates the nature of the problem. One of my philosophy professors
phrased it as follows: evil exists in the world; if God exists, there are only
two reasons for evil's existence: either He wants it to exist, or He cannot
stop it from existing; either way, He is not God. This phrasing of the
problem is a fallacy, because the concepts of good and evil are human
creations. God by definition is the reason there is something instead of
nothing. The something can be whatever God wants it to be. If this
something involves pain and suffering for His creations, so be it, it is His
creation. He can do whatever He wants with it. It makes no sense to say that
before creation there existed a requirement that God's creation must be
friendly and kind to any beings He creates. He created creation, it is what it
is. As I discussed in an earlier essay, ethics is simply a set of rules created by
those in power to stay in power. It makes no sense to demand that God be
ethical. He is the ultimate power and source of all power. He makes
whatever rules He wants. It makes no sense to talk as if He has a choice
between good or evil or wills good or evil. The concept of choice and will
necessarily involve an incomplete being that needs something. God is
omnipresent, infinite, and complete by definition. He does not need
anything, and thus there are no choices that He has to make nor for Him to
want or will anything. He and His nature all exist by necessity. As the
philosopher Spinosa described, we may just be moments in the infinite
necessary existence of God contemplating Himself and thus we have the
perception of time, choice, and will; but, it is simply human perception that

10

sees choices and will. God's existence and all aspects of His nature exist by necessity.

The problem as I have phrased it is a more accurate description because the issue is a bigger problem of morality. Given that God is the reason we exist, does He owe individual creations anything for giving us existence we never requested? Do we owe Him something for making us exist? Given all of the evil that has existed in the world, including evil inflicted on innocents such as infants and beasts of burden, even if God were to offer us eternal happiness in Heaven simply by accepting Him as He is, would it not be our moral burden to reject it? Why does God prefer certain people over others? You can call it divine predestination, class conflict, or whatever. The reality of human nature, for other than a completely solitary hermit existence, is that God prefers to have about 1% to at most 10% of humanity at any given time live much better than the remainder of humanity and to have the power of oppression over the remainder of humanity. For this small percentage of humanity, at any given time, life has meaning of their own creation. For the remainder of humanity at any given time, their meaning of life is purely to serve the meaning created by these few Powers-that-be. In the absence of such service, life is nothing but meaningless anguish. At best they are gifted with their life being short. Dostoevsky wrote a couple of great novels asking these questions, The Brothers Karamazov and The Possessed, but never answered these questions. These are questions that must be answered as part of trying to answer the overall question of why does God hate the poor.

Let us try to build on prior essays to approach this question, try to answer it, and try to see if there is an answer as philosophers not as polemics by self serving gods. The first issue that we must approach in trying to answer this question is whether the concept of morality even applies to God. Is God moral?

Why does God hate the Poor? Prologue / Part III

This next essay dealing with this question was supposed to deal with the issue of whether God is moral. However, I'm going out of context for this essay because of comments that I have received. Some still say that the question of why God hates the poor is the same as asking why God allows good and evil. It is not the same question. I'm going to use the argument for "intelligent design" as a means to further explain and differentiate why my question is distinct from and is not the same as the question of why does God allow good and evil to exist.

The argument called intelligent design is made by its proponents as an argument for the existence of a personal God in opposition to some evolutionists who argue there is no such God. Logically, in terms of the nature and philosophy of science both arguments are essentially nonsense because neither argument is scientific. Statistical analysis and correlation are all modern science needs to be science. This essay series does not deal in the philosophy of science so I will not deal with the nature of evolution nor philosophy of science but only contemplate the intelligent design argument as a means to specify and clarify the relationship between God and the poor. The argument from intelligent design is substantively unsound and a fallacy because there is no intelligent design in the universe. From the smallest part of reality and onto the largest and from the smallest event in history and onto the largest historical events, reality and history is ruled by arbitrary and random acts. Everything in life is essentially decided by luck, despite popular opinion to the contrary. For example, even supposed obvious differences in good and evil in popular opinion between a Winston Churchill, Franklin Roosevelt, and an Adolf Hitler and the events of which they were a part are not the result of any inherent differences in the universe, in their nature, or any intelligent design, but of pure luck. With a change of birthplace, parents, education, and class upbringing, the places of even such obviously different individuals in history as hero or villain would easily have been exchanged. In fact, five hundred years from now historians will treat these three as equals. If anything, historians will investigate and write about how Churchill and Roosevelt got away with their many historical blunders and outright evil acts to cause human suffering that created the power of a Hitler.

Reading, writing, or crying about genocide, fascism, Nazism, or whatever the latest fad evil political -ism may be and dividing historical individuals into heroes or villains is a shallow understanding of the absurdity of life, history, and the universe. Only those ignorant of history divide history into the good and the bad and into heroes and villains, male or female, of one race or of no race. Regardless of the majestic greatness of one's heroes or the despicableness of one's villains — be it a Churchill, Hitler, Muhammad, Martin Luther King, Nelson Mandela, Gandhi, or whoever — the historical good or evil of individuals and of social constructs is not the substance of reality. Such concepts of good and evil, hero and villain in history are purely results decided as a matter of luck and the roll of circumstantial dice. The winners in life need not ever worry about morality, ethics, or the law; such are concerns only for the losers. Simple creation of historical heroes and villains gives meaning to one's life and creates a simple morality of good and evil that ignores the banality of evil and the haphazardness of both good and evil in daily existence — that is in individual life, the only reality of which an existentialist is certain. If Hitler had died in his youth in the trenches of the Western Front or during one of the first half-dozen assassination attempts upon him, he would be remembered as a courageous recipient of two Iron Crosses who died for his country and for workers' rights — in fact, if he had died during one of those early assassination attempts upon him, he would probably to this day be remembered as a hero and martyr for socialism. In which case, Churchill — if remembered at all — would be remembered as he was known during World War I: a self-aggrandizing, dishonest, ambitious, political hack psychopath from a rich family whose fortunes he squandered and who was responsible for the Gallipoli Campaign disaster. Muhammad is essentially a 7th Century Hitler who succeeded in creating a one thousand year reich and thus as victor is a prophet instead of a villain. Dr. King and Mandela were lucky to have racism as their opponent. As exhibited by their sexual conquests of women, patrician personal ambitions, and political shrewdness to take credit for the work of others and to let others do their killing and dirty work for them, they would be just another 1984 O'Brien will-to-power conqueror if they had a more sympathetic opponent. Gandhi was a racist patrician wife-beater who was lucky to have others do is killing for him. Such individuals are not really individuals but social construct values created for marketing purposes by patricians.

The reality of history is that 90% to 95% of individual humans regardless of status in life as poor, rich, slave, free, beggar, worker, and so forth if put in the right circumstances would knowing and intentionally kill every other human being or watch idly as others knowing and intentionally kill every other human being — including eventually those watching. The only difference for the modern patricians of our Technological Society is the law allows them the power to have others do their killing for them. The individuals who make up each of these two classes of bound variables arbitrarily and randomly change each moment of life. The heroes who make up the 5% or 10% at any given moment who would rather be killed than kill another or watch another be killed will move over randomly and arbitrarily

14

as a coincidence of sometimes insignificant changes in circumstances to the other set made up of killers. Meanwhile, some of the killers will at that same moment transfer over to become heroes. Thus, the existential reality is that 100% of individuals under the right circumstances would knowing and intentionally kill every other human as a matter of brute and irrational or even rational force.

It is pure luck that has made one set heroes and the other villain. And the same is true of all heroes and villains throughout history. The real intelligent design of the universe is more analogous to a poker game in which God is the dealer, calls the games, knows the players, and sets the antes, raises, and bets. Not only does He know the players and the cards, but He made the players, who are what they are because He made them in the same way that He made the cards and thus the probabilities are what they are because He made them. In theory, giving God the benefit of a doubt by assuming that He does not cheat and by assuming quantum randomness not deterministic classical randomness, we can say He does not control the outcome of each hand nor of the game. These are decided purely by the luck of the draw, the probabilities of the given deck, game, and hands, and on each player's ability to read the probabilities and the other players. In theory, this game universe is an empirically just and fair universe in which there really is no good or evil. The best player wins and deserves to win. No one can say that it is an evil that the best player wins nor in any practical sense can we say that it is unjust that the best player wins and the loser loses.

It becomes unjust, unfair, and evil only when we bring morality into the mix and by that I mean we view the game from outside of the game. The best player, given his God-given abilities, at any given time can do nothing but win. And the worst player, given his God-given abilities, at any given time can do nothing but lose. The reality of this card game universe in which the winners and losers are set is really much worse. As the dealer, God is entitled to call the ante and to set the highest bets and raises. If He calls a big enough ante, bet, or raise, many people are excluded from playing, let alone having any chance of winning — even assuming they had all equal other abilities to win.

In the big picture of this card game universe, it does not really matter whether player A, B, C, or D wins, as long as they keep playing to keep the universe going. To make matters worse, God creates the players so that they will only play if there are winners and losers. No one who wants to play in this card game universe is going to keep playing if there are no winners or losers. Everyone wants and believes that they can be a winner until it is too late. Why would God design such a universe to favor some players over others? Of course, many noncompetitive altruistic types who may be reading this would see an easy solution to the problem: simply don't play. But that is equivalent to saying simply do not play the game of life and ignore the way the game is designed. This is easy to say if you want to live the life of a hermit waiting for Christ to return in the Last Judgment, then it's easy to say don't play the game. You are essentially choosing death. However, if you want to live, prosper, or at least survive in the real world, you have to play the game, and you have to play to win. Or otherwise, those who only care about winning take everything you have: mind, body, and soul. God is God, so there's nothing stopping him from creating such an unfair universe. But also, there's nothing stopping Him from not creating this game, so why does He do it — instead of creating a different one that is fair? Is God moral?

In the perspective of my poker game example, it seems that this question is one of justice or fairness because He treats some creations better than others, but it really isn't. Justice and fairness only have meaning in relation to a morality. Is the question of whether God is moral the same as asking whether He is just or fair? Now that you hopefully understand why I differentiate the question of good and evil from the question of why God hates the poor, I will go back to the intended next question in this series, is God moral?

Why Does God Hate the Poor: Is God Moral?

If I thought of God as another being like myself, outside myself, only infinitely more powerful, then I would regard it as my duty to defy Him.
— Ludwig Wittgenstein

Is god moral? To contemplate this question, we must have some agreement on the meaning of the words "morality" and of "God". For simplicity, I will usually use the classical "He" to reference God since I lose track of the present fad of grammatically cycling between "She" and "He" and because "It" seems to lessen the seriousness of my contemplation. Personally, I do not care whether God is a He, She, or Whatever.

I submit the meaning of the word "God" is probably easier to agree upon existentially. We have to contemplate this question in the same way one would contemplate the ontological proof of God: from the perspective of the word "God", that is of our definition and understanding of the existential meaning of the word "God". Whatever meaning that word has for anyone regardless of whether they are a theist or an atheist or anything in between, its one necessary and universal attribute would be that the word "God" by definition means the reason for their being something instead of nothing — this is true even of a pantheistic version of God in which the universe and its existence occurs by necessity or simply by luck through the workings of universal scientific empirical laws and thus these laws are your God. Agnosticism is not rational; since this is a rational contemplation, I am not dealing with agnosticism. I am therefore I think — I think in particular and especially about my existence. If I think then I think of the reason for there being something instead of nothing including there being me. It is irrational, delusional, and cowardly to fail to take a position on the reason I or anything exists.

For morality, the only attribute for its meaning that is universally agreed upon is that it is an act of will. It is an act of will giving meaning to a meaningless universe. That we "will" may be an illusion and the choices we make pre-destined or pre-determined by empirical material reality but even if such is true, all moral, immoral, and amoral choices would still be called and are acts of will or choices — free or not. Morally, immorally, and even amorally, even if I am pre-determined or pre-destined to be something, I can still reject that something. If there is no free will other than the illusion of freedom, such rejection will only be nominal and a fight I cannot ever hope to win but it is still there as a choice and a powerful one at least existentially if not for anything else. It is a choice that will define me and give meaning to the meaninglessness of my life even if it is a predestined or predetermined life because morality as the absurd hero Meursault of Albert Camus's The

Stranger finally realized as he faced the gallows is "opening [one's] heart to the benign indifference of the universe" and willing to give its meaninglessness meaning. There is a large existential difference between accepting one's fate and fighting against it — even if the fight is destined to end in loss. Remember the last words of Camus' Myth of Sisyphus; as Sisyphus looked down and contemplated his meaningless task and became conscious of his wretched condition, in this tragic moment he realized "[t]he struggle itself [...] is enough to fill a man's heart. One must imagine Sisyphus happy". (For a more detailed analytic contemplation of the meaning of the words "free will", please see Wittgenstein on the 'Illusion' of Free Will.)

As contemplated in many other essays, ethics, good, and evil are meaningless when discussing God. But what about morality? Despite His necessary nature, does it make sense to talk about God making moral, immoral, or amoral choices? Or, as Socrates asked, is something moral because God wants it or does She want it because it is moral? If the reason for there being something instead of nothing is simply the universe and you are an atheist or your God is pantheistic, it makes no sense to apply any concept of morality to God — the universe simply is, its meaning is to exist. Its existence precedes its essence and precedes language and thus any wordgame of morality. What if you have a personal God such as the Christian God Who is a Being? He is an infinite, omnipresent, and all-powerful Being but still a Being. As a Being, is He able to will the universe to have meaning and thus have a morality? At first impression, it appears that the concept of morality should apply to a personal God. However, in reaching this first impression, we forget what morality is: willing to give meaning to a meaningless universe. Even a personal God does not need to will anything nor does He need meaning; His existence is its own meaning. She is complete and whole, infinitely and completely in Himself or Herself or whatever your personal God may be and Existence is the meaning of God. Therefore, God is not moral or immoral but the best way to describe even a personal theistic God is to say He is completely amoral. I must say the "best way" or seems because as with the pantheistic God, this existence that is the essence of God also precedes language and thus logically and strictly speaking is something "whereof one cannot speak, thereof one must be silent".

God being amoral or the wordgame of morality not applying to God makes perfect sense as Wittgenstein's famous quote above brings out. If God were really just another moral busybody or even the most powerful moral busybody of all telling me how I should be living my life in the short span I have in life, He is no better than any other moral busy body except in degree not in substance or essence. He is no better in quality than any other existentially created morality that makes my life simply a mascot for its sense of morality; I might as well create my own morality and enjoy being a god myself.

That should answer the question as to whether God is moral for all concepts of God, except for Christianity and its Trinity or any equivalent form of theism or polytheism. I suggest that the theologians of the early Church came up with the Trinity concept as a way around the amoral nature of God. As always, the ancients were a lot smarter than what we give them credit for being. Since the Trinity includes a person who is human, Jesus Christ, the question of His morality must continue. Given that Jesus Christ — the Jesus Christ Person in the Christian God — is human, is Jesus Christ moral? Regardless of what one might think of Him, there can be no dispute that He is moral. According to the Christian concept of what Jesus Christ is and then on to the Beatitudes and on to anything that can be ascribed to him, this Christ Person does want to give meaning to life and does not exist simply as having the power of His Existence be its own meaning and an end in itself. According to the Trinity dogma, there is a Third Person, the Holy Spirit, that is the relationship between God the Father and the Christ Person. So for a Christian with Faith, the answer is that God, through Jesus Christ, is moral. God loves us, wants us to be happy, will reward us in heaven for following his morality, so on, and so forth. At this point, we are leaving rationality and getting into Kierkegaard's existential Leap to Faith and of Pascal's Gamble that are beyond this essay.

However, the Trinity problem does not solve the initial question we are asking. So far, there is no problem with the use of words. Like the ontological proof, we are dealing with logically subtle and abstract but sound and valid reasoning derived from the very meaning of the words and concepts used. Morality is an act of the will, not of reason. Morality is an individual willing meaning into the world. And thus, evil is the opposite of whatever this good the individual defines to be. God, in the non-Christian sense is amoral because God just is. The Christian option seems to be that in exchange for accepting as a necessary part of God's amoral nature all the suffering that has been, is, and will be part of humanity — in exchange for accepting that — we will be rewarded with happiness in heaven by the human person in God: Jesus Christ. By accepting the massacre of the innocents, I will be happy. Such beliefs do give meaning to life and thus are a morality.

But it is not one with which I want to be involved. Or, morally should be involved? Why not? Because it is unfair and unjust — it is not a fair and just way of getting results. So what? Again, it is God's universe. He can do with it as He or She pleases. Why do I not want to be involved in it? Is it altruism on my part or arrogance and conceit? Is it because I want to have greater power than God? Since God is amoral, is He also unjust and unfair? I will consider these questions next.

Why Does God Hate the Poor: Is God Just?

Is God just? Can the words "justice" and "injustice" be applied to God? The search for justice has been a constant source of injustice in life, especially for the poor and working class from whose perspective we are examining the question of "why does God hate the poor". Calls for justice are usually the starting stage of the greatest injustices of history. "Justice" has been defined in many ways, by philosophers and theologians, all of which have failed to achieve justice. For classical and for modern philosophers varying from Plato to Karl Marx, justice means "from each according to his abilities, to each according to his needs". As usual, this sounds nice in the abstract, but both for Plato's Republic and to the other extreme of Marxism and its post-modern progeny, the end result in reality is always the same tyranny of the few over the many that is the class struggle of history. Modern theorists on justice, such as John Rawls in his books A Theory of Justice and Justice as Fairness and Karl Popper with his book The Open Society and Its Enemies, tried to subsume the Christian Beatitudes into a secular form of social norms but such attempts have failed miserably in making any qualitative improvement in human society. When acting in association with capitalism and science, some calls for justice have at least materially or quantitatively improved the human condition. However, such association qualitatively has served only to replace chattel slavery by wage slavery; all have done nothing to improve qualitatively human nature in any way in relation to any concept of justice or injustice — all such concepts are relative to a given point in history. The lower classes continue to remain slaves and will continue to do so for as long as there continue to be humans in the class struggle that is history.

The word "justice" is purely a human creation. In the reality of human language, the meaning of most words is their use and usefulness. In this sense, the meaning of the word "justice" in human reality as used by any individual is "that which gets me what I want". If the individual wants something to give their life meaning and they get it, the process and result is just. If someone else or something denies them this meaning, this denial is unjust. Assistance in getting what the individual wants in order to give meaning to their life is justice. Any denial is unjust. For a society, justice is anything that maintains order and the status quo power structure of that society, and injustice is anything that threatens the status quo power structure and order of a society.

Does the word justice have any inherent meaning when applied to the concept of God? Again, you must remember that God is defined here as the reason why there is something instead of nothing. Based on any purely analytic examination of the nature of God, the answer to the question of whether justice or injustice applies to God is "no". God is the ultimate power of reality. He can do whatever He wants, whenever She wants, and to whoever He wants. The word justice has no meaning when applied to God, any more than do the words good or evil. The concept of justice does not apply to God and He cannot be described as just or as unjust. Nothing can deny God anything. God does not need anything. God does not owe us anything.

This is why religions such as Islam and Old Testament Christianity that make justice the ultimate virtue and aspect of God are so dangerous in life, especially to the working class and the poor, more so than religions such as New Testament Christianity that make love the ultimate virtue. Any religion that gives the attribute "justice" to the absolute power that is God is a dangerous illusion for the working class because it equates the workers' or the poor's need for something with God's need for something. This equating of what the worker wants to what God wants not only weakens workers' ability to will, work, and fight for what they want and need because they expect God to get it for them but also serves to justify any atrocity that the individual worker wants to commit to their fellow workers in order to get it. This results in the working class wasting a lot of time and energy fighting among themselves while the Powers-that-be stand by and watch the battle — enjoying their power. Once one starts to believe that God will give you prosperity, education, or whatever simply because one wants it and therefore it must be just, one has lost the battle against the Powers in any struggle one is fighting. God may do such for the rich and powerful, but He will not do it for the working class or for those that are not among the Powers-that-be; this is the whole point of this question we are asking of "why does God hate the poor". He plays favorites. He is entitled to do so. Workers and the poor must work, fight, and struggle for what they want. He is not just or unjust. He is God, He can do whatever She wants.

New Testament Christianity tries to get around this aspect of God by talk of love, mercy, the Trinity that includes a Person that is divine, and so forth trying to make love the primary and only attribute of God. However, even according to New Testament Christianity, justice is not a reality in this life and, from my reading of the New Testament, is not a reality in the next either — if there is a next. "Justice" is a minor word in New Testament Christian reality. I realize the New Testament states in the Beatitudes "Blessed are those who hunger and thirst for righteousness, for they will be filled. And Blessed are those who are persecuted because of righteousness, for theirs is the kingdom of heaven", but these Beatitudes do not say how the thirst and hunger will be filled nor what the reward will be. It definitely will not be by justice because God can do whatever He wants with His creations, either in this life or in the next, if there is any. As Clarence Darrow said,

"There is no justice in life, in or out of court." More accurately, the description should be that there is no justice in this life or the next, if any.

This Christian reality is best brought out by the Parable of the Workers in the Vineyard at Matthew 20:1–16 that goes as follows:

> *For the kingdom of heaven is like unto a man that is a householder, which went out early in the morning to hire laborers into his vineyard. And when he had agreed with the laborers for a penny a day, he sent them into his vineyard. And he went out about the third hour, and saw others standing idle in the marketplace, And said unto them; Go ye also into the vineyard, and whatsoever is right I will give you. And they went their way. Again he went out about the sixth and ninth hour, and did likewise. And about the eleventh hour he went out, and found others standing idle, and saith unto them, Why stand ye here all the day idle? They say unto him, Because no man hath hired us. He saith unto them, Go ye also into the vineyard; and whatsoever is right, that shall ye receive. So when evening was come, the lord of the vineyard saith unto his steward, Call the laborers, and give them their hire, beginning from the last unto the first. And when they came that were hired about the eleventh hour, they received every man a penny. But when the first came, they supposed that they should have received more; and they likewise received every man a penny. And when they had received it, they murmured against the goodman of the house, Saying, These last have wrought but one hour, and thou hast made them equal unto us, which have borne the burden and heat of the day. But he answered one of them, and said, Friend, I do thee no wrong: didst not thou agree with me for a penny? Take that thine is, and go thy way: I will give unto this last, even as unto thee. Is it not lawful for me to do what I will with mine own? Is thine eye evil, because I am good? So the last shall be first, and the first last: for many be called, but few chosen.*

Faced with injustice, essentially God's answer is: "it is my world [vineyard], I can do what I want with it and with you".

So just to summarize where we are as of now in our contemplation of the question of "why does God hate the poor", we can conclude that this question is not one of good or evil, of morality or ethics, nor of justice or injustice. None of these human creations apply to God. If He wants to hate the poor, He is free to do so without any limitation by attributes of good, evil, morality, ethics, or justice. What about fairness? Also, is it a matter of free choice? Is God choosing to hate the poor? Does She know She does it?

23

Does God love and hate? Can She really hate the poor? Or, is His mistreatment of them purely business and not personal? I will consider these questions next.

Why Does God Hate the Poor: Is God Fair?

Is God fair? I ask this question because fairness and its use seem to connote a different meaning than justice, so much so that the present ruling class glorified philosopher John Rawls wrote a book entitled A Theory of Justice arguing a rationalist foundation of "justice as fairness". Fairness implies a certain simplicity and mathematical balancing that appear to be much more accurate and honest than the concept of justice. For example, if you have three starving people and three apples, fairness would dictate that each person gets an apple. If you are playing football, you expect the referee to be fair to all players, that is by applying the rules and making the calls the same for all players.

This type of reasoning creates an illusion of rational rules that creates an illusion of justice but ultimately, when critically and analytically examined as they pragmatically work in reality, it still leads to the same uses and usefulness as the words 'justice' and 'injustice' contemplated in prior essays. For example, if you try to factor into the three-hungry-people-decision the different ages, weight, metabolism, health, and almost infinite number of other factors that differentiate people, it becomes a rationally unsolvable problem of "justice". Do you give a young, fat, healthy child, with a much more likely chance of survival more than one apple or the sick, skinny old person who needs it more but most likely will die anyway? The same types of problems arise in the football example. If a player is viewed as an asshole, especially playing in an away game, the fans expect more calls to go against the player and the calls will go against the player more often. Such unfairness in the rules — or such unfairness in the application of rules — is actually seen as justice, punishing the player for being an asshole (however the Powers-that-be or the fans define being an asshole). So much so that if the player is seen as an asshole because of actions off the field when not even playing football, such as for example he beats his wife, then the fans, the league, and the referees expect that the player will not even be allowed to play but will be suspended or thrown out completely out of his playing job and salary. Thus, in this latter case, the Powers will deny the player, his wife, and their family any income from the only employable skill the player has and bankrupt them as an act of justice. Such unfairness in the game is seen as justice in society.

Ultimately, as with justice, anything that helps get the individual or social group ruling class ideology what they want as meaning in their life is fair and also just. What hinders that goal is unfair and unjust.

Therefore, in substance, analytically, there is no difference between the use and usefulness for 'justice' and 'fairness' and neither can be applied to the concept of God. If He wants to give three of his starving creations three apples, one apple, zero apples and just watch them starve to death, or whatever She wants to do with the apples, He is free to do so unhindered by any human created concept of fairness. Ultimately, the answer to the question asked by Socrates of whether something is good, fair, or just because the gods' love it or whether the gods love it because it is good, fair, or just is: neither. If we were to answer this question in terms of human language treating God as a Person, the answer would be that something is good, fair, or just because God loves it.

Do our questions regarding God's hatred for the poor apply also to nature and the animal world, in essence to all of reality or just to humans?

Why Does God Hate the Poor: Is It a Universal Hate?

Why does God hate the poor? Is this a universal hate? As we contemplate the issue of God's hate for the poor, all of our answers so far have negated possible explanations based on human excuses for hate that cannot be applied to God. The meanings of "good", "evil", "morality", "ethics", "justice", and "fairness" are all human constructs, created to give us meaning in life. None of these words can serve as an explanation, justification, or excuse for God's varying treatment of His creations. The individual creates a morality to give meaning to life and a social group creates an ethics to maintain the group's power structure. "Good", "evil", "justice", and "fairness" are all terms that describe other humans or things in reality that either help or hinder our created morality or ethics. These words do not apply to God, God can do whatever He wants and is not limited by our concepts. None of these human words explain why God prefers some humans over others. How far does this preference go; does it go beyond humans? The question of God's hatred for the poor, is this question limited solely to humans? Do concepts and questions such as these that we are asking apply only to humans? I've been treating them as such, but in order to avoid confusion about what we are contemplating, I want to be clear that the issue of God's hatred for the poor is not simply a human issue but one of the natural order of reality and of all life.

I will clarify what I'm doing by using an example that I recently came across. A bunch of Yale University economists, with the aid of anthropologists and other academics, have been using an island of monkeys near Puerto Rico for social experiments. One test involved giving the monkeys pretend money that they could exchange for food from one of two persons. One person would show the monkey a cup with one grape but in exchange for the coin would give the monkey two grapes. The other person would show the monkey three grapes but then in exchange for a coin would give the monkey two grapes. So in both situations, the monkey would get two grapes. As you would expect from academics not skilled in analytic thought, the Yale professors using illogical or unsound assumptions went on to make a series of illogical conclusions. The unsound and illogical assumption they used was that the rational thing to do would be to take grapes randomly from either tester since the end result is the same — one will always wind up with two grapes regardless of which tester one picks. However, the monkeys almost universally always picked from the tester who showed one grape but gave them two. The Yale academics went on to make the unsound and illogical conclusion that the preference was irrational and that this universal irrational preference is ingrained and explained in the monkeys by, as always, the universal academic religion of evolution. Reason abhors arbitrariness and randomness.

Without getting into the philosophy of science and theory of knowledge at issue, based simply on clear logical reasoning that I've been trying to delineate in these essays and not on the prejudice and bias of academia, hopefully you will see how irrational their conclusions are and what they miss in terms of learning and knowledge from their experiment. Imagine having an employer who offers you one of something in exchange for doing a small job. You then do it and he gives you two of that thing. Imagine another employer who offers you three of something in exchange for the same job. You do it but then he gives you two of the same thing instead. In both cases, for the same job, you get paid two grapes. So given the choice of employers next time, for doing the same job, which employer would you choose? The rational choice is the one who gave you the extra thing, not the one who took away one of the offerings. Playing the odds and appearances, the one who gave you something extra, based on your needs and desires for as many as possible of whatever is being offered, appears to be the more trustworthy individual; that is, appears to be the person most likely to give you what you want and thus from the rational perspective is the person who is more moral, ethical, just, and fair. Since you know the other person will most likely take at least one thing away, they might take more away given the chance and thus there is a greater danger of their denying you what you want. So why give that cheat a chance? Based on the facts and rational concepts of good, morality, justice, and fairness, the rational choice is the person that adds a thing.

In reality, both of the Other may be scientists who may one day kill you to autopsy your brain regardless of the rationality of your choices. Until then, the rational choice is to pick the one giving you the extra thing based on concepts of morality, justice, ethics, and fairness and good and evil or whatever rational analysis is used for the choices. The human rational concepts of good, evil, morality, ethics, and justice and fairness based on getting what one wants are universal, not only to monkeys but to all life. There is a natural law in the universe: anything that gets us what we want is normatively what ought to be. Even at the level of quantum physics, the randomness of nature disappears once an observer is added and when observations get large enough. At that point, the randomness disappears and deterministic classical physics kicks in and everything appears orderly and beautiful. At that point, you can read The Consolation of Philosophy by the Roman philosopher Boethius and you can be impressed by the beauty and order of the universe and then concepts of good and evil and other norms start to make sense.

The difference between humans and monkeys and other non-human life is that we can be irrational. Instead of always acting in our rational best interest, we can reject the rational choice of the tester that gives an extra grape and, irrationally, instead pick the other tester intentionally: out of spite; rejection or protest of the testing situation; to mess with Yale testers; out of hope that the other tester will give us all three grapes; or out of an almost infinite number of reasons for acting irrationally — whereas there is usually only limited reasons to act rationally. As Wittgenstein's Rule Following Problem conceptually analyzes, unlike computers, monkeys, and other entities, there is no such thing as "rule following" for humans other that a specific instance of following a rule — we can always create new rules and not follow those we create or already have.

As humans, we can look outside the game and ask the question that other life cannot ask. Why does God hate the poor — including poor monkeys and the uncountable number of other lives and beasts of burden varying from abused animal prey to worker bees dying for a queen out there who have lived and live their entire existence only as a struggle to exist or are forced to live their existence in servitude to the Powers who not only control them but decide whether they are to live or to die. So this question we are asking, of why does God hate the poor, is important not just relative to us but to all of reality that is unable to ask it.

Why Does God Hate the Poor: Does He Know and Think About This Hate?

Why does God hate the poor? Does God know He hates the poor and does He think about it? As we contemplate the issue of God's hate for the poor, you must continually remember and keep in mind what our concept is of God. It is the God of the ontological proof: God is the answer to the question of why there is something instead of nothing.

As shown by Descartes, other than the knowledge of our own existence while conscious of it and the ontological existence of God, we have no rational knowledge we can call truth as that word is classically and usually defined: knowledge about the world that is indisputable in all possible worlds. All rational truths are pragmatic and the word "true" is merely a "syncategorematic term" as called by the Scholastics as the philosopher Hilary Putnam sarcastically calls it. For example, saying "it is true the car is green" does nothing to the sentence "the car is green" other than allowing us to transition from talking about green cars to talking about sentences about green cars. Twentieth Century philosophy has successfully shown that the old distinction between synthetic and analytic truths in reason is no longer valid nor sound. All rational knowledge is ultimately synthetic. That is, its initial foundation is in our consciousness and perception plus our sense experience interaction with the world and our intentional synthesis of the struggle between these two forces.

This is even true of mathematics that used to be considered an example of undisputed analytical truth that is true in all possible worlds. Despite the protests of rationalists and idealists and of philosophers and most mathematicians who say they discover mathematical truth independently of the world, the reality is that no one discovers or has discovered mathematical truth a priori or simply by thinking about it without sense experience interaction with the world as a foundation for that discovery. Geometry came into being as a result of the need for ancient Egypt, Samaria, and other ancient cultures' need to measure and describe land for tax and sale purposes. Algebra came into existence based on a need for traders on the spice routes to keep track of their accounts. Reason is a tool for solving perceived problems. Once this tool develops basic rules for solving problems, through induction and deduction or other logic, it can derive an infinite number of variations and inferences from those premise rules to become analytic knowledge or tautologies that are true in all possible worlds once the initial premises are accepted. But such does not change the initial synthetic nature of that knowledge that can change if the assumed premises are changed.

Reason is the mind's tool for solving problems. Truth and

31

knowledge only exist pragmatically. If a statement works to solve a problem, it is true until it stops working, at that point it becomes false. Scientific statements can only be proven false but never true. That is why they are scientific statements instead of statements in practically any other field that are never proven either true or false.

However, reason is not the only possible source for knowledge. We know it is not because reason contradicts itself when it makes a statement as I just have that it is absolutely true that all truth is relative. By stating such a conclusion, reason states there is absolute truth and contradicts itself. Reason, unless dealing with pragmatic truth, always winds up contradicting itself and therefore proves it cannot achieve knowledge of any truths other than pragmatic truths. We exist, therefore we think. Once we know we exist, then through the ontological nature of such existence we know God exists: a reason for there being something instead of nothing. What about God? Does He know things in the same way we do, purely by interaction with the world and the need to solve problems caused by that interaction? Does She exist, therefore She thinks? Does She reason to solve problems while thinking of Herself and while perceiving reality?

We cannot ontologically apply the meaning of the word consciousness to God in the same way that we apply it to ourselves or to the animal world or to any life. We are not a necessary being that is the reason for there being something instead of nothing. He is. God is. We exist, therefore we think, because we may not have existed before and we may not exist later. It is possible that we think while not conscious of existing. For example, we know there exists something we call subconscious thought that we cannot talk about. Is a misnomer to call it "subconscious thought". Since we cannot talk about it, it is not really thought. Thought and language are the same thing. "When I think in words, I don't have 'meanings' in my mind in addition to the verbal expressions, language itself is the vehicle of thought." — Ludwig Wittgenstein. It is simply one of those things "whereof one cannot speak, one must be silent" of Wittgenstein. However, we never are silent and always try to talk about it anyway because it is so important in life. Without talk, we know it by action. It is often pragmatically better and faster than conscious thought, such as when athletes go into the zone and become the ball or whatever they are doing or when mathematicians come up with intuitive creative proofs out of apparent nothingness.

However, for us to know we exist, we must first exist. This is not the state of affairs of God. His existence and knowledge of His existence cannot be separated. Otherwise, He would be in the same position or in the same state of affairs as us and will need a reason for existing instead of not existing —

which would be God. So for humans, the knowledge or absolute truth we have is that if we exist then we think, that is, the logical statement if a then b. For God, knowledge is simply the principle of identity. Existence equals thought, a = a. Unlike for us, in which all knowledge is synthetic, God's knowledge and thought are all analytic.

The best way to view this problem is to go back to our earlier poker game example. Reality is a poker game in which God created the cards, bets, ante, game rules, and thus all the probabilities and created the players and then let things play out. In substance, He is not the game and does not control the outcome, though in essence He is the game because He can do or He can think all the probabilities and knows how the players will play and thus the winners and losers and the eventual outcome. The players are desperately trying to figure out what hands will be played but never can figure it all out. That is why life is a gamble. The players are in the game therefore they think synthetically. They induce and deduce to try to win as they are destined to try to do. Meanwhile, from the first ante, God standing outside the game knows every hand and outcome because He can analytically figure them out. He knows it all while simultaneously the entire time the players are ignorant of the outcome.

This concept is beautifully expressed in the prologue to the Gospel of John. "In the beginning was the Logos and the Logos was with God and the Logos was God." Logos is the word from which we derive our word logic. In some translations, Logos is written down as "Word", "Word" is used for Logos. Either way, whether you use Logos or Word, this prologue is consistent with our ontological proof for the existence of God and is a beautiful shorthand expression of it.

So does God know He hates the poor? Yes. Does God think about hating the poor? Yes, in the sense that He knows about everything. Knowledge and thought are the same with God, always analytic and tautological in the mind of God.

The next question is the Will of God, the Will of God is something that religion is always talking about. Does God will His hate for the poor?

Why Does God Hate the Poor: Does He Will This Hate?

Why does God hate the poor? Does he will His hate of the poor? Almost universally among continental philosophers, they see the human will as the driving force of human nature. Among many it is also the driving force and even the substance and essence of reality. For example, the idealism of Hegel with its dialectical logic of the spirit of history eventually became both the world concept of the fascists and the material class struggle of the communists. For Schopenhaurer, man's will was the substance and driving force of reality. For Friedrich Nietzsche, it was the will to power that was a driving force of nature and humanity. Even the leap of faith that is the basis for Kierkegaard's Christian theology was a leap of the will. Existentialism depends on the will to give meaning to the meaninglessness of the universe in which existence comes before essence. However, other than the concept of ethics, there is probably no word that is more distorted and practically meaningless in the working class perspective of life — which is the perspective of these essays and this blog.

The word "will" as it is usually used and for which it is useful and therefore as is its meaning cannot be applied to God. Theological talk treating the will of God and free will as if they were the same type of word is one of the biggest cons by theology on the poor and the working class. To will something requires one lacks it and wants it. God is omnipresent, all powerful, and the source of what there is instead of nothing. He needs nothing. He is complete and whole, always was, is, and will be. Therefore, this meaning of will cannot be applied to God as an omnipresent all-powerful being because She does not need anything.

"Will" however also describes wanting to continue. At least for the moment, I am alive and want to continue living instead of committing suicide. This existential reality is different from wanting something such as meaning for my existence: the will that leads to hope. As Friedrich Nietzsche said, hope is the worst of all evils because it prolongs the torments of man.

However, at least this concept of will involving only existence does not entail lacking something and therefore, at least in theory, can be applied to God. Or can it? If God exists and continues to will his existence, such implies that He could commit suicide by not willing to exist. Ontologically, this seems to be a possibility. God got the poker game of the universe going but do we need Her around any longer to continue its existence? He is the reason there is something instead of nothing, but now that there is something, does the something need Him to continue? The Dealer calls the game but can we now change the dealer?

We are forgetting in this paradox our philosophy of language reality and getting caught up in our own words. These questions ignore the ontology that we are talking about because they assume or imply God acting in time. We exist. We continue to will our existence. One day we may not exist. We exist in time. Time is our relative perception of the possibilities around us and their coming to life around us. God does not exist in time. He is omnipresent by the definition of the concept of God, that is why we have the ontological proof for Her existence. The something that is now includes time because we our conscious of it and perceive it and thus create changing relationships based on our needs, but God has no needs and is the source of time and therefore is outside of time. By the definition of God, if She existed in time then we would have to ask why is there this something god in time instead of nothing. That would lead us again by necessity to the reason there is something instead of nothing: God — outside of time. Time is a meaningless word when applied to God.

Everything is a "now" to the God of the ontological proof — there is no past or future. The concept of will only applies nominally to God in the sense that He is the reason there is something instead of nothing. He wills the something and continues it by definition. But this use of "will" is not will in the sense of a choice. A choice would mean that God has options between one thing or another, that He is incomplete in some way, that He exists in time in some way. Only incomplete beings have options or choices because they are incomplete. That is not ontologically possible for the concept of God. As the ontological proof goes, God is the perfect omnipotent omniscient originator of the universe, the reason why there is something instead of nothing. There is nothing God lacks requiring a will for it. God does not exist in time, so He cannot will existing now and not later or vice versa. Thus, whether He wills the poor and His hatred for them are meaningless questions that only apply nominally to the question we are asking. Nominally, God does will the poor and His hatred of them in the same way that He wills all creation: by necessity.

In summary, we have reached a point of having numerous answers. In our contemplation of the question of why God hates the poor, we know that God knows and thinks about the poor and His hatred for them in an analytical completely ontological sense and wills it in the sense that His will is also his existence and by necessity the existence of something instead of nothing. The poor and His hatred of them are a necessary part of the something for which He is the reason that exists. Also we have been able to conclude that neither justice, morality, ethics, or fairness bars such hatred of the poor. The poor and God's hate of them exists necessarily but why? Why not love them necessarily?

Before we go further to answer the question of why, there is the question of hatred itself. What does hate mean? Does God hate in the same way we hate? Does God love in the same way we love? Could He love the poor instead of hating them and treating them in the way He does? These will be our final questions on this issue.

Why Does God Hate the Poor: Can God Love? Part I

Our consciousness and perception of reality reveals that God hates the poor. Can He love them instead? Can God love? All Western religion including secular religions such as humanism state either and usually both that God is love ot that love is the greatest virtue. Do either of these popular statements withstand critical analytical examination? Not really. This hype about love, especially by religion, serves to keep the poor happy and the working class in their place.

In my reading of history — for that matter in any reading of history — love such as love of country, power, money, tribe, and even love of family and love of justice have caused much more evil and suffering in the world than hate. Hate has rational limits. Few, if anyone, would risk their life for hate. Almost all who have or who can love would risk their life and that of others and outright kill others for the love of whatever it is they love. Hate may make you a serial killer of 30 to 40 people but love will make you a patriot willing to kill three to four million. Love is not necessarily a good. That conclusion seems to depend on what you love. Love of power is supposedly bad. It is considered bad for the poor. The Powers love the poor and oppressed but only if they are willing to stay poor and oppressed. The Powers worship love of power as a good despite sometimes pretending otherwise. Regardless, love of power is what drives human culture because history is class struggle, so pragmatically love of power may be called the ultimate good in terms of human culture surviving the power of the natural world always trying to kill us. Capitalism at least admits it considers love of power a good — as long as there are equal opportunity and struggle among the Powers which there never is.

Loving your neighbor — now called "the Other" by secular religion that wants to hijack Christianity without the Christ — as you love yourself is supposedly a good but what about the first necessary premise of that command: love yourself? In order to love your neighbor, you must first love yourself since your existence is your only certainty. However, self-love seems to be one of the most harmful evils that has caused just as many atrocities as love of power if not more. Then again without self-love, humans would have died out millennia ago. The ability to love oneself blindly regardless of any faults and thus to have hope for a better life is what allows the poor and working class to survive its miseries and the ridicule of the Powers around them constantly trying to demean their life. Supposedly, according to women at least, love and sexual love are distinct and being addicted to the first is good but being addicted to the latter is bad. You will have to ask a female philosopher to explain that difference.

What a mess this love issue is. In order to determine if God can love, we must first define love. We must first see if we can ontologically define love especially insofar as that word is used in respect to God. Self-love just as consciousness and my existence is one of the few items in the fabric of knowledge that are ontologically certain; we either have it or do not. Thus, we can ontologically — not just pragmatically — rationally contemplate self-love. As long as we exist and are conscious, regardless of what skeptical reason may say, we know and perceive self-love otherwise we would commit suicide. The Commandment to love your neighbor as yourself is more of an attempt to get humans to reduce their self-love than to raise their love of others. There is no doubt as to the existence and strength of self-love, so I will start by contemplating and defining self-love to see through the cultural and social smokescreens created to make self-love a vice for the working class and to replace it with all sorts of hype such as God is love or love is life in order to keep the poor and working class in their place.

The most basic element and requirement of a person having a use and of the usefulness for the word love and thus its meaning in self-love are that the person wants to exist and wants to continue existing. Love is an act of will saying I want to exist and want to continue existing. This does not seem to do it though. If I want to exist living as a heroin addict on the streets of New York earning money by being a prostitute, the conclusion would not be that I love myself but the exact opposite: that I have self hate and am trying to destroy myself. Just wanting to exist would not give much meaning to the expression "love your neighbor as yourself". If I want to live as a prisoner in North Korea and want the same for my fellow humans, again, the implication is that I neither love myself nor my neighbor. Love seems to demand more than just existence.

Our present United States culture would say that the additional element that self-love demands in order to be love is individual happiness: that we want or will a happy life for ourselves — we have hope. And, thus, when we love others, it also means that we want a happy life for them. This emphasis on happiness seems to be nonsense and a modern cultural phenomena. For much of the world, individual happiness is not a possibility. Never was and never will be. That is why we are asking the question that we are asking. Yet all these people that really have no hope for happiness in life are still able to love themselves and love others. There is more to life than happiness. My favorite example of this need that goes beyond happiness in life is expressed by the eight points of the Maltese Cross establishing the required moral standards for the Knights Templar: faith, repentance, humility, fairness, mercy, forthrightness, honesty, and suffering. Happiness is not in the list of elements for self-love by these warrior monks. Of course, these eight virtues only have power and meaning because the knights expected happiness in the afterlife after giving up on happiness in this life. So we are back to the point that perhaps this additional element is happiness or a want or hope for happiness.

Some philosophers, such as for example Thomas Aquinas, have in fact concluded happiness as a required element for love: love consists of a desire to exist, to continue existing, and to want happiness. Happiness for Aquinas consisted of an afterlife with God. So as to the elements that define self-love, can it be be defined as a desire to exist and to continue existing plus a hope for happiness?

I do not think so. The greatest love is the love of one who sacrifices their life for another such as the soldier who falls on the hand grenade to suffer the entire blast then dies so that others may live. This act of love most certainly did not demand a desire or hope for happiness in this life. It is not clear it demands or requires a hope or belief for a happy afterlife. In the ancient world, the Greeks believed in an afterlife that consisted not of an eternity of happiness with a loving God but with Hades — the word from which we get our word hell. A life after death for the Ancients was simply to exist in a peaceful sleep with one's ancestors unaware of any past or future but just peace after a life of struggle and war. Despite such a dismal view (from out modern perspective) of the afterlife, this view did not stop the Greek warriors at the battle of Thermopylae from sacrificing their lives to try to save their neighbors. Actually, those so called pagans with their belief in a Hades apparently had more love for their neighbors than modern Christians have either for their God or for fellow Christians. The Ancients fought to save their neighbors. Modern Christians with barely a whimper allow the modern warrior religion of Islam to tramp around killing Christians so as to trample out Christianity.

So maybe the third element that defines love is not a desire for individual happiness but a desire for the happiness of others. This would make some sense and explain a lot because as rational beings we know that the individual dies and always will die. Any hope for humanity to continue must be for humanity to continue not for any individual to continue which is impossible. But, now we are reversing ourselves on the logic. Love of neighbor cannot come first and cannot define self-love. As even the Christian Commandment admits, in order to love your neighbor, you must first love yourself. Ontologically, we know this must be the case. We have to stay focused on the ontological nature of the knowledge we are seeking. I only have true knowledge of my own existence. Everything else could be a figment of God's imagination as idealists argue.

Love of neighbor must start with love of self. In order to define love, we first have to define and understand what love of self is. So back to square one. Love of self we know involves at least wanting to exist and to continue existing — the desire to continue existing plus a desire for something more. The something more is the open issue. The something more is not only the final element that defines love but is also the element that from the social perspective makes it a good or an evil; and, in the case of self sacrifice love, it is able to negate the first two existential requirements of existing and to continue existing. The only characteristic that I can contemplate that would satisfy these purposes is meaning. Self-love is: 1) the will to exist; 2) the will to continue existing; 3) plus the hope that my existence has meaning. If I find a meaning for my existence, that hope becomes real instead of just being hope thus the first two elements can be negated and I can fall on the hand grenade to save my comrades as an act of love. To love our neighbor as ourselves is to want them to exist, to continue existing, and for their lives to have meaning. If we decide on what that meaning is, it can negate the first two existential requirements for love.

Further, just as finding a meaning for life will allow for our self sacrifice of our own life for that meaning, love will allow us to want to kill and actually to kill our neighbors as an act of love to maintain that meaning. Thus, ontologically, love is: 1) the will to exist; 2) the will to continue existing; 3) plus the will that our existence has meaning. Love of neighbor or love of money is all the same ontologically regardless of whether ethics or morality calls one good or the other evil. This definition may not be very romantic or live up to the hype that love seems to have in popular culture, but that does not make it any the less true or less powerful. It is powerful enough for a person to sacrifice their own life for others. It is also powerful enough for a person to sacrifice others for that love.

What about hate? What is hate? Before we decide whether God can love the poor, I want to go on to define hate and then also see if there is a third option just as there is with morality: can God be amoral? Is there an option between or outside of love and hate?

Why Does God Hate the Poor: Can God Love? Part II

"The mind has a thousand eyes and the heart but one. If the light of the whole life dies, then love is done." So goes the poem by Francis William Bourdillon. Yeah. Right. Love always gets the good press and hate the bad, but in reality, especially for the poor and working class, hate is often a much more useful tool for survival in life than love. If the love of the Powers-that-be had their way for me, I would still be in the Navy spending at least half my life at sea risking it for their safety. Or worse, I would be working as a janitor back in my hometown or somewhere else as a poor humble servant of God in society while they run around gathering as much power as they can for themselves, for their children, and in the end still go to heaven. Religion and the Powers-that-be love the powerless, weak, and oppressed as long as they stay powerless, weak, and oppressed. Rationally controlled anger, hate, aggression, and ambition usually do more to help one work out of the working class or out of poverty than love unless you are some type of a politician, prostitute, or other willing to sell your soul for money and power.

I recently saw a documentary about Bob Gibson, a great baseball pitcher from the 1960's whom I remember when I was a kid as someone who pitched with anger and aggression and did not hesitate to use a beanball when a batter was crowding the plate thus creating a high intimidation factor with batters. He blames his anger on racism. Yeah. Whatever. Racism is as good a reason as any to hate. Even if that were true, then racism is the best thing that ever happened to him. Without the anger, aggression, and ambition to defeat the Powers that racism gave him — unlike those who accepted it peacefully and tried to change it with love by turning the other cheek — he would have been just another wannabe fastball pitcher playing in sandlots somewhere with millions of others — black, white, or whatever — with nowhere to go. Everyone playing baseball loves the game, it is the skilled hatred of losing that gets you into the major leagues. Anger, aggressiveness, and competitiveness are what gave Gibson the ability to make it and survive in the major leagues as it does for any professional player. Anger, aggressiveness, and competitiveness are each accepted as a good for the Powers-that-be and as a necessary attribute of successful capitalism but somehow these attributes are seen as an evil for the poor and the working class. They are supposed to be humble and accept their lot in life. Racism breeds hate, but the rationally controlled returned hate and the fear it creates in the Powers — just as with class struggle — can beat it and eliminate it by making the Powers who breed racism too scared to promote it.

So what is hate that it gives it such a bad rap? Now that we know what love is, defining hate should be easy. It is the opposite of love.

Self-hate is wanting not to exist nor to continue existing and having no hope of meaning in that existence. Once all three of these elements come together plus the opportunity to put a bullet in your head or in the head of others, suicide will shortly follow unless one of these elements changes. Hating others is wanting them not to exist, for them to stop existing, or that there be no meaning for their existence.

No ambiguity here. Hate, unlike love, is not ambiguous but is very clear and provides clarity for life. It is this clarity that makes hate such a useful tool in trying to survive and battle the Powers, if one can control it: that is avoiding having the three elements of self-hatred come together to the point of suicide. Unlike love requiring that one love oneself before one can love others, hate allows for the option of living while loving oneself but hating others. It is a much more versatile tool than love. One can will to exist, will to continue existing, and hope and have meaning for one's life and thus self-love while at the same time hating others: 1) willing that they do not exist; 2) that they do not continue existing; and 3) that they have no meaning for their life. In fact, hate of others could act as the meaning that provides the third element for one's self-love. So for love, you must love yourself before you can love your neighbor. But for hate, there is no need to hate yourself before you can hate your neighbor. You can love yourself and yet hate others. Hate is one side of coin with love the other.

So can God love? Or, more importantly given our topic, can He hate? Before we go on to those issues, I want to deal with some ambiguity in my contemplation and contemplate whether there is a third option between love and hate: indifference or amorality to both.

Why Does God Hate the Poor: Can God Love? Part III

As a result of our contemplation of the question of why does God hate the poor, we have been able to define love and to define hate. Self-love is an act of the will by which it states I want to exist; I want to continue existing; and I hope for meaning in my existence. Once meaning is found, love is the pursuit of that meaning, and it can negate the first two elements. Once we have self-love, we can love others or things: that is we want them to exist; to continue existing; and to have meaning in life. Hate is the opposite of love. Hate is an act of the will stating that someone or something should not exist; should not continue existing; and should not have meaning in life. In order to love others or things, one must first have self-love because our existence is the only certain existential knowledge, but self-love does not necessarily entail love of others or things. One can love oneself yet hate.

Does this result mean that living with love or hate are the only options for human life? Pull out one of the three elements of love and we no longer have love neither self-love nor love of others, but we do have something. We can continue to exist without love. The same is true for the elements of hate. Something of this existence can be seen in the character of Meursault in Albert Camus's story The Stranger. This character has given up hope for meaning in life and, therefore, does not love either himself or others. At certain points of the story, he has given up on the second element of wanting to continue to exist and lives in the moment of existence. Thus, he is not bothered by the death of his mother nor by a murder he committed without thought and without hate nor about his own impending death. He does not have self-hate nor hatred of others. He does not go beyond the moment. He has neither love nor hate. He lives a life without passion we would say. It is an existence without passion. Many theologians say that such human existence is not possible: that he is the lukewarm of the New Testament. As Jesus said in the New Testament, "So then because you are lukewarm and neither cold nor hot, I will spit you out of my mouth."

It may be true that a Christian life without passion is not possible, but it is certainly possible for life overall. It is probably the way animals look at life, without love or hate of it, that is without passion. As long as Meursault is conscious and approves of his momentary existence — that is he is conscious and perceives what is necessary to live physically — he can continue to exist this loveless and hateless life. Such an existence in fact may make him closer to our God of the ontological proof than any loving or hateful human being would be. He has his own existence and is satisfied with it. This type of existence is what God is: Her existence is Her meaning. I have defined God as the reason there is something instead of nothing, but it may be that He is nothing more than that. The universe definitely exists in this way without need of meaning and without need of passion. By just existing with an indifference to all and to all he does, Meursault is more in one with the universe and more in one with the wholeness of the one or the oneness of the whole or whatever it is the Buddhists say than anyone who loves or hates. The problem with Meursault existing solely in the moment without passion of any kind is that his life cannot lead to love, morality, good, justice, or any normative statements. At the same time, however, it cannot lead to hate, immorality, evil, or injustice. Furthermore, this indifference has its own eternity:

> *Death is not an event in life: we do not live to experience death. If we take eternity to mean not infinite temporal duration but timelessness, then eternal life belongs to those who live in the present. Our life has no end in the way in which our visual field has no limits.* — Ludwig Wittgenstein at §6.4311 of <u>Tractatus Logico-Philosophicus</u>

Concepts such as morality and ethics only come into existence when we accept the second element of love by wanting to continue to exist, and thus we need to create social norms to give us power to protect our existence. Living in the moment, one would not need ethics. One would not need morality. One does not need love. One does really need anything except one's own existence and the physical means to maintain it. There may still be the will to power, but that is an issue for another day. Both love and hate have three required elements. Pull any of these out and you no longer have love or hate. But, there is something. There is a passionless existence; it is an existence consisting solely of the individual and the will to exist. A passionless existence without love or hate is still an option for human existence.

But is it an option for God? In which one of these states does God exist: love, hate, or indifference? I have framed the question at hand as one of God hating the poor but if it turns out He cannot hate the poor because he does not hate, it seems that I may be asking a meaningless question. I do not think so. The facts of reality establish that God hates the poor regardless of what my ontological reasoning may imply because this may be a matter of which we cannot speak rationally. I will have to contemplate this issue further. For now, on the issue of humans living a life of indifference, I end with a quote from Buffy the Vampire Slayer made by Angelus during the time he lacked a soul:

> *Passion. It lies in all of us. Sleeping. Waiting. And though unwanted, unbidden, it will stir, open its jaws and howl.*

It speaks to us, guides us. Passion rules us all, and we obey. What other choice do we have? Passion is the source of our finest moments, the joy of love, the clarity of hatred, and the ecstasy of grief. It hurts sometimes more than we can bear. If we could live without passion, maybe we'd know some kind of peace, but we would be hollow empty rooms, shuttered and dead. Without passion, we'd be truly dead.

Why Does God Hate the Poor: Can God Hate?

Now that I have ontologically defined love and hate and have considered the option of living without either, what about God? Does He love, hate, or exist in a passionless existence without either?

God by ontological definition is the reason there is something instead of nothing. So the element of existing and continuing to exist must be present. If He were to hate Himself, there would have to be another reason why there is something instead of nothing and that would be God. So we are back to the ontological proof of God's existence. As discussed earlier, as an omnipresent, omniscient, complete being, She exists by necessity and thus is Her own meaning. Therefore, She does satisfy the three elements of love but only nominally in the same way that She has a will as we discussed earlier. He has to love Himself in the same way He has to will His existence. He nominally wills and loves. Just as God wills by necessity as a source of something instead of nothing not in a human sense of willing or wanting something we lack, God ontologically must love Herself because She must. God cannot hate Herself as humans can and do. This means that She cannot be passionless. Even if God does not hate, there will always be self-love in God. The more interesting question is can He hate others. He cannot hate Himself, but what about the something that He has created?

If we are all just thoughts in the mind of God, as some idealist and the pantheistic philosopher Spinosa and many Ancient and Eastern philosophies say we are then we should all share and know of the self-love that God has. In which case, I would not be asking the question that I am asking. However, I am asking it, and it is clear that God loving Himself is not a love present in all living things, at least not in humans. God's self-love seems to be present in animals and in non-human life because they do not commit suicide nor suffer consciousness and perception of a meaningless existence. So in nature, the natural world and non-human life seem to be a reflection of God's love and always have God's self-love whereas humans on the other hand not only can lack it and contemplate suicide but actually lose it and commit suicide.

As I stated earlier, we can contemplate self-love rationally because our individual existence is the only knowledge we have. I know I exist simply by existing; what else exists rationally requires evidence or proof. When we go beyond existential attributes of our existence, we start contemplating matters "whereof one cannot speak thereof one must be silent" however we cannot because these are important matters. I will try to do the best I can without becoming fiction or pure aesthetics by not abandoning the three classical rules of logic: identity, non-contradiction, and the excluded middle. To say that we cannot speak of something is a contradiction because we are speaking about it. Thus logic to a limited extent is able to speak about that which it cannot speak but only to a very limited extent as we have been contemplating. However, if this ontological language violates these basic rules of logic, then just as for other logical statements, the language cannot be knowledge ontologically or otherwise and we are getting into aesthetics.

Since God must love Himself, if we are really just thoughts in the mind of God, this love should be evident in all of us. It clearly is not. The reality is and it is factually undisputed that God hates certain people, in particular the poor, and that this hate even extends to animals and other creations while He loves others. In reality, it is factually undisputed that He prefers certain lives to exist, to continue existing, and to have meaning and thus loves them while others He hates. So as much as I admire Spinosa, we have to reject his pantheistic view of reality.

It seems in my initial card game analogy is more accurate than it appeared to be at first. Somehow God, the reason there is something instead of nothing, set up the cards, card table, antes, and players; got the game started; and now is sitting back outside the game watching to see how it all ends though He knows how it all ends. God does love nominally. Furthermore, since reality establishes that He does hate, God does hate but not Himself. Somehow God was able to create something and then remain outside of the something created. How can He do this? On this question, we have truly reached an issue whereof one cannot speak thereof one must be silent.

However, the answer of how He does hate does not matter to a question of why He hates the poor. He can and does.

The concept of the Trinity just as polytheism — breaking up the reason there is something instead of nothing into many reasons — might have been created by Christian theologians and the rational mind of the religious as a way to get around this essentially amoral nature of God. God knows He is amoral as He knows everything. In order to reach an understanding with His human creations, God becomes human so on and so forth and this requires a Holy Spirit to mediate between the two. Does this Trinity and polytheism generally help us in any way on this issue of God's hate of the poor? Not really, hate for the poor is still hate for the poor, but I want to discuss this option as a side issue for a moment before I continue with my questioning and contemplation.

Why does God hate the Poor: Who are the hated Poor? Part I

I need to step back a moment from the progression of this contemplation to clarify or define in some clear way who are the poor to whom I am referring so in case anyone reads these contemplations we are contemplating the same people. The only way I can make sure we have the same meaning of "the poor" is by exemplifying how I use that word and its usefulness to me. As I tried to clarify in other essays, though it is a good start to define the poor workers simply in terms of material poverty or as wage slaves, this is a very narrow view of reality. Many of the poor in the United States would be considered well-off materially in many other places in the world. Somewhere in the world, on average, every 15 seconds a child dies of preventable diseases including many resulting from malnutrition or contaminated food or water. Furthermore, qualitatively, as every historical study of the issue confirms, measuring relative to the material quantity or economies of their respective times or era, there is little material difference between the lives of workers stuck as wage slaves their whole lives in modern Technological Society and the lives of chattel slaves in past societies. It is still true as it has been true for much of the past millennia that 1% of the world still control approximately 80% of the world's material wealth; we are all materially better off because the 100% is so much larger. There is still a lot of material and physical poverty in life but this concept of the poor is incomplete.

It is easy to start with a material definition of the poor, but it is a mistake to define or connote the poor solely in terms of material or physical poverty. This type of definition relying completely on material poverty is not my definition nor is it the definition of Western theology when it says that we will always have the poor among us by which they mean both the materially poor and what they consider to be the spiritually poor. It is usually not even the definition used by atheists or other non-religious, at least not for those who have the empathy to go beyond their own delusional will-to-power to declare God dead so that they can replace Him with whatever new god they want to worship — because they lack the courage to rebel and reject God honestly. Good existential writers such as Kierkegaard, Camus, Dostoevsky, Herman Melville, and many other writers include among the poor those destined to have lives of powerless absurdity. Good existential writers are able to empathize with such a state of affairs. However, my concept of the poor is better brought out by considering how bad existential writers describe the lives of those who live in absurdity — bad existential writers such a Frederick Nietzsche and Jean-Paul Sartre and his girlfriend Simone de Beauvoir.

Consider the story of Nietzsche and the Turin horse. Supposedly toward the end of his life, Nietzsche was in Turin, Italy when he happened to see the driver of a horse drawn wagon whipping a horse to get it going. Nietzsche was so moved by this scene that he ran to the horse, hugged it around the neck, and started crying. His friends and family members had to physically force him from the horse; he had an emotional breakdown; and he then spent the remainder of his life in his mother's apartment being cared after by his mother and his sister. The moral of this story according to the loving readers of Nietzsche is to establish what a sensitive person Nietzsche was and thus by implication show the subtlety and sensitivity of his writings and thus the subtlety and sensitivity of his loving readers. Yeah, right; why did not Nietzsche or his loving readers ever ask what happened to the horse and driver? Like Nietzsche, did they go on to spend the rest of their lives cared for by their mother? The movie Turin Horse by the Hungarian director Bela Tarr asks this question and his answer is they went to work and continued to work the rest of their lives. The driver and the workers are the poor of my question. Nietzsche and his loving ethically superior Dorian Gray worshipers are the rich.

Technological Society has replaced the horse by mechanical devices and thus has saved millions of horses from living a life of struggle serving humanity by denying them life since we no longer need horses. However, Technological Society did not do the same for the wagon driver; they are now Uber drivers and the struggle of life and class struggle continues as it must for history to continue.

Sartre in his Being and Nothingness describes inauthentic and authentic living as a dialectic of freedom. As an example of inauthentic or bad faith living, he describes a waiter who is "play acting" at being a waiter. He is not complaining the waiter is being too patronizing, phony, or fake such as being overly polite and flattering to get tips but is actually complaining that the waiter is being too good at being a waiter. According to Sartre, being a waiter is just a social construct. It is not really what anyone really is and one should not see their self-identity or identify as being a waiter. According to Sartre, identifying oneself as being a good waiter is an means to deny one's freedom; it is a means to replace authentic self-identity with a social construct because one is afraid of the freedom to be whatever they want to be. Thus, finding meaning in life as a really good waiter is an inauthentic life.

For Sartre and for many of his existential followers, the waiter is denying his freedom by trying to become a social construct. What Sartre is actually exemplifying — as did his girlfriend Beauvoir — is "play acting" at being a philosopher. If the waiter had the luxury to do so, the waiter most likely would live authentically writing pretend philosophy books while sitting in cafes drinking wine with his other writer friends and his girlfriend

52

ridiculing those who are trying to do their job of serving them as best they can. Problem is the waiter does not have that option, he must work for a living and see meaning in that work. The waiter is the poor; Sartre, his girlfriend, and their worshipers are God's beloved.

As I contemplated in other essays, as Wittgenstein's Private Language Argument brings out, there really is no such thing as self-identity defined by a private language of an individual person. Language is a social construct and thus once we leave areas of pragmatical truth such as science, all descriptions are social descriptions not private ones. The poor and the workers who are the poor in my question do not have a choice of "self-identity"; they are what society says they are. They can fight against their social identity and try to change it but it is a fight they will lose and must lose because they do not control the strategy, tactics, armament, or the field of battle. Society and those who rule it control those and must. The Powers are those who have the power to control what ought to be and what ought to be said about what ought to be. Sartre and others like him have the power to define the waiter as inauthentic, play acting, or whatever normative description they have the power to make; the waiter is stuck with what life gave him. The Powers construct their own social identity and then like Sartre look upon hoi polloi around them as cowards who lack the courage to live authentically after having defined what it means to live authentically.

Thanks to the material progress provided by science and technology, we are likely to reach a point in the foreseeable future where material and physical poverty will not exist. Everyone will have the basics necessary for materially and physically having a healthy individual life and perhaps with only robots instead of other humans as servants. This future will result from the past suffering of billions of dead souls — approximately 15 souls for each one of us presently living. Is such future happiness worth the price paid by those dead souls? As Camus and Dostoevsky specifically write, who would dare to assert that eternal happiness can compensate for a single moment of human suffering? The same question can be posed for human happiness in this life. These writers used the example of suffering babies and children and even of purely innocent beasts of burden such as donkeys, mules, and horses who from birth are destined to live lives of struggle for their human masters and then die a lonely death as the lonely animals they are. Dostoevsky's description of a man beating a horse to death in Crime and Punishment and of the hunting dogs killing a child in his book The Brothers Karamazov are examples that are hard to forget. If these books are too long, try the short stories of George Orwell such A Hanging, Shooting an Elephant, and Makaresh dealing with real-life events that he witnessed. These fictions and stories pale in comparison to real-life tragedy such as the siege of Stalingrad. The Powers of this future will accept happiness based on such a price. More likely, just as social justice warriors do now, they will accept their happiness not upon unity with the past or with a sense of loyalty to their fifteen souls but upon a Dorian Gray sense of moral superiority condemning the past as if it was made up of human idiots and assuming they could have done much better.

Are the Powers-that-be willing to accept the massacre of innocents as the price to pay for their eternal happiness? Yes, they are. That is why they are the Powers-that-be. The Powers build their happiness upon the past even when condemning the past so as to control the future: to control what ought to be to make a world in their image. The poor are those that cannot accept such a deal or are not allowed to do so or not even given the choice to do so.

Do not get me wrong. I am not ridiculing such a future. Personally, the so-called dystopia of Aldous Huxley's Brave New World is a better world than we have now and better than most of the world that I have seen during my life. Given a choice between being materially rich but spiritually poor or being materially poor but spiritually rich, in my experience most people that have known physical poverty would choose being physically rich over spiritual richness. The reality of life is that money can buy love and happiness both in this life and in the next, but on its own love will only get you hate as the love/hate coin flips. However, this brave new world of the future for which my ancestors and I have fought and struggled to achieve, is it really worth what it took to get there? Does not seem worth it right now. The price for ending physical and material poverty seems to be workers who have lost the will to fight and are viewed as inauthentic waiters by those who also lost the will to fight but do not need to fight.

This is the substance of the problem and the nature of the definition of being poor and hated by God. God so hates the poor that the rules of the card game are set so that either the poor must endure the absurd meaninglessness of no physical and material power over their lives or endure the meaninglessness of a lack of a will to power for their lives while the chosen few Powers-that-be enjoy both material and normative power not only over their lives but over the lives of the poor. For most of humanity, it is either material poverty or spiritual poverty. It is one or the other. This is free will? This is worse than no choice at all. In the future, the poor will be defined not by material poverty but by a poverty of will; it will still be poverty.

God can do whatever He wants. She is doing it. So why does it bother me? Is it really envy that is my problem as the Bible says in the Parable of the Workers? Is it what Nietzsche called resentment: the herd's envy of their betters? Should I just accept my fate in life? This is the final issue that I must face in defining and clarifying who are the poor in my question of why does God hate the poor.

Why does God hate the Poor: Who Are the Hated Poor? Part II

According to Christians, by reference to such concepts as the Sermon on the Mount and the Beatitudes, they argue that their God of the Trinity through its Second Person Jesus Christ as human may have the option to hate but has always chosen and will always choose to love humanity because He is one of us. He needs the Third Person of the Trinity the Holy Spirit to act with the God of the ontological proof that I am contemplating. It may be that the entire concept of the Trinity was created by Christian Theologians to deal with the question of hate by the God of the ontological proof. This serves as a final exemplification of my concept of the poor in my question at issue.

As usual, Christian arguments — as with any religious, ethical, or moral argument — depend on a careful picking of dogma and, for Christianity, of biblical passages while ignoring others. Because it exemplifies God's hate of the poor, one of my favorite biblical passages is Matthew 20:1-16 known as "The Parable of the Workers in the Vineyard". This Parable goes as follows:

> For the Kingdom of Heaven is like a landowner who went out early in the morning to hire workers for his vineyard. He agreed to pay them a denarius for the day and sent them into his vineyard.
>
> About nine in the morning, He went out and saw others standing in the marketplace doing nothing. He told them, "You also go and work in my vineyard, and I will pay you whatever is right." So they went.
>
> He went out again about noon and about three in the afternoon and did the same thing. About five in the afternoon, He went out and found still others standing around. He asked them, "Why have you been standing here all day long doing nothing?" "Because no one has hired us," they answered. He said to them, "You also go and work in my vineyard."
>
> When evening came, the owner of the vineyard said to his foreman, "Call the workers and pay them their wages, beginning with the last ones hired and going on to the first." The workers who were hired about five in the afternoon came and each received a denarius. So when those who came who were hired first, they expected to receive more. But each one of them also received a denarius. When they received it, they began to grumble against the landlord. "Those who were hired last worked only for one hour," they said, "and you have made them equal to us who have borne the burden of the work in the heat of the day."

But he answered one of them, "I am not being unfair to you, friend. Didn't you agree to work for a denarius? Take your pay and go. I want to give the one who was hired last the same as I gave you. Don't I have the right to do what I want with my own money? Or are you envious because I am generous?"

In this Parable, the Jesus Christ Person of the Trinity admits to the hateful nature of God and sees no problem with it. God as the vineyard owner is being an unjust, unfair, and hateful boss to the workers who spent all day working hard for Him in the hot sun, but according to God, so what? It is His vineyard and His money. He can do whatever He wants with it — which is true. What is funny or sad about this Parable is that this portion of it admitting that even the New Testament God is unjust, unfair, and hateful is ignored by accusations of "envy" against the workers who simply wanted a fair distribution basis of equal pay for equal work for their wage slavery to the vineyard owner. Usually this Parable is taken as a lesson against envy: the workers who worked all day and expected to be paid based on the work done for their work were envious of those who got paid the same for doing less work. This is envy?

Maybe they are envious, so what? They should be envious. Is it envy for the vineyard owner to want as much money or more money for his grapes than those of the other vineyard owners? No. Is it envy for the vineyard owner to try to maximize the profit of his vineyard so that it makes as much or more than the other vineyards? No. Is not envy, greed, and a will-to-power some of the necessary foundation motivations of capitalism, the best economic system that we have available at the present time? Is not envy such as is exhibited by the vineyard workers what gave workers in history the aggression to form unions and fight for a fair distribution of wages giving us such benefits as the 40 hour week and weekends (that we are gradually losing as we lose unions)? If it is envy to want equal pay for equal work, then I do not see how envy is much of a sin. Why does the Parable only lecture the poor about envy as a vice? It would be a waste to lecture the vineyard owner for owning more land than he and his family can work; civilized society would break down if such excessive ownership were to be a vice.

If Christians are going to argue the Trinity as a way to get God's love back into the card game of reality, one must also have to admit that it may be the Trinity is the reason why the love of God was out of the card game in the first place. If God was really just one Being and reality is pantheistic with this Being, we would all by necessity know equally all of His love. Since He is not but includes supposedly a human Person, this human Person may be the means by which God stays out of the card game of

58

life. Regardless, this is a side issue, and we're definitely getting into areas whereof one cannot speak thereof one must be silent and getting away from my question of why God hates the poor. Again, He is God. He can do whatever He wants — as the Parable of the Workers admits. If He wanted, He could have started all the workers at the same time. He could have created shift work so all the workers worked the same amount of hours. He could have created some kind of pay system where everyone gets equal pay for equal work. As an all-powerful God, there are an infinite number of things He could have done. He did what He did, and does what God does. At least in our reality, He clearly hates the poor and treats some who live in this reality different, better or worse, than others. Whether there are possible worlds with different realities is a question beyond this blog.

I seem to have reached a point at which I should be finally able to answer the question. I have contemplated the ontological nature of God — Her relationship to justice, fairness, morality, ethics, good, evil, love and hate. Time for an answer.

Why does God hate the Poor: The Answer

I have finally reached the point of being able to answer the question that I am asking: why does God hate the poor? I have defined the nature of the God of the ontological proof and contemplated the issues that come up when trying to understand why He hates the poor. I have either resolved those issues or defined them as necessary so that I can answer the question.

The answer as to why God hates the poor turns out to be very simple, and it goes right back to the ontological nature of the God of our contemplation as the reason there is something instead of nothing. He hates the poor because He can. He is the ultimate power and can do whatever He wants. In fact, since She acts by necessity, She must do whatever She wants. If you could choose your acts and had the power to do whatever you want, you would choose to exercise the power to do whatever you want. God acts by necessity, not from incompleteness requiring choice. He is what He is and can be.

It sounds as if we are getting into matters of which one cannot speak logically and wherefore one should be silent. Given the importance of this issue and the time spent on contemplating it, I want to keep in mind that logic is not the end-all tool for truth and illusion. The logical mind is creative and imaginative and can use fictional analogy as a means to reach truth and illusion when logic reaches its endpoint for either. Through logic's creativity and imagination, I want to clarify my answer to the question I am asking by going back to the Parable of the Workers in the Vineyard and my card-game analogy. The Parable is a good description of my answer to the question except for two facts: 1) it describes an agreement between God and the workers; 2) the Parable assumes free will.

The Parable justifies God's hate of the workers who worked all day for him by saying they were offered a deal to work all day for a denarius, accepted the deal, got the deal, and therefore have nothing to complain about. That is not a true analogy of life, especially not for the workers of the world. God, the vineyard owner, not only creates the vineyard and similarly the cards of the game of life but also created the workers, players, pay, ante, vineyard, game, and the work needed to be done and knows better than anyone the hands or the work at the end of the day. He designed the pay scale and odds so that only a small percentage of people will win at the expense of many others, and He knows who the winners will be and who the losers will be. To say that the workers freely made an agreement, contract, deal, or whatever, or that they knew they were making a contract, deal, agreement, or whatever is an absurdity. It is outright deceit and dishonesty that shows theology and Christianity at its worst. If the workers had known that God would be paying the same amount to the workers who did nothing all day, they would have waited until then to accept an offer to work. The fact is that they did not know what He would do until He actually did what He did. They could not know it because He can randomly do whatever He wants, whenever He wants.

Free will to deal with God, if it exists, is reserved for those few with the power to enter into contracts with God, not for the poor who can not or have only an "I live or I die" choice to accept the power of God and His work in His vineyard.

That is why I am asking this question in the first place. The choice to work in a vineyard or not to work is an "I live or I die" choice for workers. If this is how Christian theology, or any theology, defines free will then maybe there is free will for workers but otherwise there is none. More likely, free will does not exist in making a choice to live or die but only in accepting or rebelling against your destiny and fate in life. There is no reason, justification, or any rational basis for God's hatred of the poor — it is simply an exercise of pure power — and thus we can accept it on the same nihilistic basis or rebel against it through our own nihilism. God is the ultimate nihilist, but workers can at least be nihilists in our rejection of God's nihilism when we finally know of it. As Spinoza argued, knowledge that we are not free is the ultimate freedom.

George Orwell ends 1984 with the character Winston ending his "self-willed exile from the loving breast" and accepts death not with rebellion but with tears realizing, "[i]t is all right. Everything was all right. The struggle was finished. He had won the victory over himself. He loved Big Brother." The Powers-that-be try to make power seem to be some kind of inhuman evil to be avoided. It is similar to those people with a lot of money saying money is not everything or does not buy you happiness. It is the essence of humanity to seek power but such search is seeking for God. This is true of all reality — organic or inorganic, matter or energy, or whatever fiction is used to describe and try to control reality. The search for power is the search for God, either to be with God or to become a god. And it cannot be avoided if we are living humans. If the New Testament ended at the crucifixion, there would be no Christianity and no Christian saints who reject all worldly power. It ends with the power of the Resurrection: The promise of unity with the ultimate Power of this and all worlds.

I have answered the question at issue, in large part but not completely. When I started this contemplation, part of my questioning was what do we do with the answer? Given God's hatred of the poor, what do we the workers do about it, if anything? What should God be doing about it, if anything? In the presence of the indifference of the universe, what difference does the answer make? Paraphrasing Dostoevsky and Camus, should we accept the hope of a reward from God of happiness as compensation for a single moment of human suffering? Or, as the ultimate act of human power against the random power of God, should we spit in His face and reject God and thus become a god ourselves — not by being the reason for there being something instead of nothing as God is, but by being the reason for there being nothing instead of something. Nietzsche ridiculed that humans rather wish for nothing than not wish at all. What is the ultimate victory over the hate of the universe to our existence: to accept our fate and be free through the knowledge we are not free; to wish for nothing though we do not control satisfaction of the wish; or to stop the wishing?

This is not an ethical question that can be answered by society. Society, controlled by the Powers-that-be, will always choose the power of wishing. Essentially, the Powers will always choose to continue their Power over others in a search for power as an end in itself — this is how they find the God that loves them. Ethics is a set of rules created by those in power to stay in power. This remaining issue of what to do about the reason for God's hatred of the poor is a moral question, to be answered by any individual who can ask it. This moral question has its own unique set of problems that I need to contemplate.

Why does God hate the Poor: Does the Answer matter?

Does it really matter why God hates the poor? No one else seems to care. The vast majority of people have and always will spend their lives trying to survive and gain as much power as they can during their life — as they should do. So, why does the answer as to why God hates the poor matter to me and to some others?

In deciding whether God or I should do anything about this hatred of the poor by God, the answer to the first part of the question is easy. Because God gave me this life I never asked for, does God owe me any duty to do anything about how messed up this life is? Given our contemplation so far, the answer should be obvious: No. He is God and does whatever He wants to do consisting of acting by necessity. According to Christians, God did do something. He became human through His Son Jesus Christ. I will leave that response between you and Søren Kierkegaard and go on to the question of what my response or duty ought to be regarding God's hate for the poor.

Why does the answer bother me so much? What, if anything should I do about this ontological truth that there were, are, and always will be the poor in life who will be the object of God's hate? The answer does not matter to those God loves nor should it. Unfortunately, it does not matter to most of the poor. As worker's rebellions varying from Spartacus to the French, Haitian, Russian, and many other revolutions have shown and as most of history in general has established, poor people given the chance are just as greedy, homicidal, hateful, power-hungry, and generally what we call evil as any rich and powerful person can be or are.

As Camus said: "The slave begins by demanding justice, and ends by wanting to wear a crown." The undisputed fact of reality is that the poor, if given the chance, will seek the same power over me as the few powers-that-be already have over me. Christian saints claim to love others as an end in itself but that is bullshit. Take away the promise of the power of the Resurrection and they would be no different than anyone else.

So, why should I care about these poor as I defined them previously physically, materially, or spiritually? "F__k them," should be my answer. I should just worry about myself and my own search for power so that I become a power-that-be; so that I become among the few beloved by God. This is the reality ignored by even the existentialist writers, from Camus to Dostoevsky, Kierkegaard, Herman Melville, and so on. They see the reality of what is but ignore the potential for much worse when reaching their conclusions of absurdity and hopelessness. They go to the edge of the abyss, look over, and then step back. That is why, in the end, despite their claims of despair, hopelessness, and absurdity, they always end with hope and avoid nihilism.

They start with phrases such as by Camus, "Everything is permitted. It is not an outburst of relief or of joy, but rather a bitter acknowledgement of a fact." Or by Dostoevsky, "If there is no God, everything is permissible." But after saying this, they back off. All of a sudden, they start writing about good and evil as if those terms have meaning outside of whatever random meaning an individual or the powers-that-be arbitrarily give to them. Why do they back off of it? Are they cowards? Is this all part of God's playing with His hatred of the poor, to create false hope to hide His hatred of many of us?

The dead are dead. There is nothing that I can do to help them. Even if they were alive, they should really not mean much to me. Based on my life experience and reading of history, at any given time, considering both the reality and potential of human nature, 90% to 95% of humanity is divided into four kinds of humans: 1) those who would walk into gas chambers to die when ordered; 2) those who would do the ordering; 3) those who would do the killing; and 4) those who would clean up afterwards. The remaining 5% to 10% of humanity, at any given time might refuse all four.

Are those remaining the ones that are troubling me? Am I in that 5% to 10%? The problem with this percentile division or categorizing of humanity is that those who make up any of these categories at any given time are completely random. It varies from time to time, depending on the circumstances. So, today's gas chamber victim may be tomorrow's executioner. Today's hero may be tomorrow's coward. The same is true for me. This is all part of God's hatred for the poor. Any one of us, depending on the circumstances, could fall into any one of these categories.

In some ways, being poor is a great excuse for going through life, once you reach maturity. Many advocates for the materially poor complain about the loss of opportunity. Among the poor, there may be a wasted Albert Einstein, Nelson Mandela, or whoever might exist, and we are wasting their potential. Well, also among the poor might exist a future Joseph Stalin, Adolf Hitler, or whoever. If these two, for example, had stayed poor and in poverty and died young, it might have been the best thing that ever happened to them and to the world. At least if you died as a victim of the gas chambers, you will be remembered with pity and kindness. That might not have been true if you had actually had a chance to live.

One's status in life as hero or villain is purely random for the vast majority of humans. So, the poor themselves are not a reason to care about them. In his book, The Confessions, the so-called Church Father St. Augustine stated, argued, and essentially realized that even babies are either evil or have the potential for it. He exclaims to God, "No one is free from sin in Your sight, not even an infant, who's span of early life is but a single day." As St. Augustine explained, "What, then, was my sin at that age? Was it perhaps that I cried so greedily for those breasts?" That is, of his mother, for milk. "Certainly, if I behave like that now, greedy not for breasts, of course, but for food suitable to my age, I should provoke derision and be very properly rebuked. My behavior then was equally deserving of rebuke." He complains that once he saw a mother with two babies, who, while trying to feed one, the other cried out of envy and jealousy for his turn at the trough. This is a tough view on life in a tough era in which some theologians, including St. Augustine, even argued and believed in the damnation of unbaptized babies. As a true power of this world and apparently of the next, St. Augustine accepted this condemnation of even babies as the price that he had to pay for eternal happiness for God. What a great human being he was.

It never occurred to him to rebel against such happiness and to rather accept damnation and hell with those babies. So, why should it bother a sinner such a me? And why does that rebellion occur to me as a viable option? In terms of the potential evil of humanity, of even babies, his contemplation was right. Why should he reject his happiness simply because some — maybe as little as 5% of those dead babies — could have been true saints of humanity if given the chance? The differentiation between the lives of those who fit into the 90% – 95% of humanity that I describe as random poor and those in the remaining 5% to 1% that are the powers-that-be are just as random.

The chosen few that have the power to decide for themselves into what percentile they will be, and furthermore, to what percentile the remainder of humanity will be, are chosen randomly. It is a random choice by God. As a random choice, it could have been me placed into any one of the four categories. It could have been me — depending on luck deciding whether I was a gas chamber victim, operator, rebel, or a St. Augustine — deciding into what category the remainder of humanity will be.

So, do I care and have empathy for the poor and hate the powerful as purely a selfish act — as an act of envy — because I am not among the powerful as St. Augustine was; if I had that power, would I not care in the same way that he did not care? Probably. Unlike the existentialists who in the end pretend their concerns are not based on their own self-love but are based on empathy and a concern for humanity, the truth is that their concern and my concern is mostly a selfish act of envy and jealousy as described or as alleged in the Parable of the Workers.

Well, so what if that's the true motive of my concern? God's power includes the ability to randomly decide whether He would give me life and what kind of life. He has randomly decided to allow his chosen few to control my life and most of human life. Why should I accept his randomness? He wants me to work all day for the same amount of money as those whom He chose to work in His vineyard for only an hour. Why should

I accept that? There is no reason why I should accept it, just as there is no reason why not. By randomly rejecting God and His random choices, I am getting as close to being a god as a human can become. Without that, the only other option for being a god is making a choice to randomly make nothing out of something: killing life. Killing life, the only random act that is even more God-like but for some reason that I cannot choose.

I can try to do better than God's random power. I cannot do better since I am not God but I can at least try to do it. I do not want to accept happiness based on the suffering of babies because by doing such — I say to myself — I would be accepting His arbitrary power over me. I reject His power. Tough talk. But, as we used to say in the Navy, I can talk the talk, but can I walk the walk?

Why Does God Hate the Poor: Virus Supplemental Part I

The individual is in a dilemma: either he decides to safeguard his freedom of choice, chooses to use traditional, personal, moral, or empirical means, thereby entering into competition with a power against which there is no efficacious defense and before which he must suffer defeat; or he decides to accept technical necessity, in which case he will himself be the victor, but only by submitting irreparably to technical slavery. In effect he has no freedom of choice. — Ellul, Jacques. "The Technological Society". Vintage Books: N.Y., N.Y. (1963) p. 84.

The last few weeks of mass hysteria have been a rich source of contemplation for me. Some of which will be covered here. Part of this series of essays will be an "I told you so" since I rarely in life have a chance to express this sentiment and never expected to see my prior predictions come to life in my lifetime. Part will be a supplemental contemplation on my primary concern throughout these podcast essays: what freedom if any do wage slaves, slaves either materially or spiritually, have while ruled by the gods of Technological Society? The latter contemplation has been further enlightened by my being stuck at home with the time to re-read a book I last read in my childhood: All The King's Men by Robert Penn Warren (Houghton, Mifflin, Harcourt: N.Y., N.Y. 1996). In the years since my first reading of it, I gradually lost faith in fiction as a source of anything but aesthetics serving more to hide reality than reveal it and thus completely forgot that this novel has my most favorite ending of any novel I ever read even though I completely disagree with the meaning expressed by this ending:

> *The creation of man whom God in His foreknowledge knew doomed to sin was the awful index of God's omnipotence. For it would have been a thing of trifling and contemptible ease for Perfection to create mere perfection. To do so would, to speak truth, be not creation but extension. Separateness is identity and the only way for God to create, truly create, man was to make him separate from God Himself, and to be separate from God is to be sinful. The creation of evil is therefore the index of God's glory and His power. That had to be so that the creation of good might be the index of man's glory and power. But by God's help. By His help and in His wisdom.* All The King's Men at pp. 658-59.

The above simple expression describing in its simplicity a meaning upon which some theologies have written entire books of verbiage and yet

69

have failed to express with such beauty is to be admired regardless of one's opinion of its value. It is truly a work of art in its purest form created from words. The essays collected here have been a conceptual contemplation of the social conversion of chattel slavery into wage slavery and its implications for those who are the new school slaves of Technological Society. Unlike mainstream modern and post-modern philosophy and theology who criticize this social construction while being instrumental in creating and maintaining it, I have accepted it as a necessary attribute of Technological Society. Class struggle while hopeless and ultimately destined and fated to be a loss for the individual fighting its power is necessary so we can all be a "victor" in the ultimate struggle we all share to survive the indifference of the universe to our survival. If you choose life, you necessarily choose Acceptance of your social class in life and the struggles it entails. For the individual who does not allow themselves to be cheapened into an aesthetic struggle between a fictional Self and a fictional Other, this struggle necessarily entails nihilism as a metaphysics and as a morality.

The following is a thought I expressed in my first published book Existential Philosophy of Law and further highlighted in subsequent writings:

> As George Orwell wrote in 1984, in order for the Powers to keep their powers, it is not enough for hoi polloi simply to accept Big Brother, they must love Big Brother. Through law and its Powers, our Technological Society is bringing to life O'Brien and his Room 101, but it is not a room with a rat cage but a sterile, pleasantly decorated, warm, friendly room with a surround sound of legality and illegality negating conscious, complex tragedy in the classical sense: replacing it with fear, hatred, and the joy or pain of either winning or losing but without dignity of emotion nor deep or complex sorrow and thought while at the same time denying the truth that 2 + 2 by definition makes four.

As a result of recent events, even after this virus debacle is over, the present and future for wage slaves will be living and working in a Room 101 more commonly known as "WFH" (Working From Home) with all the necessary pleasantries and attributes for making such bearable. In the past, there was a differentiation between house slaves and field slaves. The future of class struggle is a differentiation between WFH wage slaves and the field wage slaves who will be serving their needs. The overseers who make up the Outer Party class will still exist to assure these two groups of slaves are busy fighting each other so as not to bother the Inner Party. So, uh, I told you so.

Such WFH future will be more than bearable, it will be

pragmatically better in almost every way by which such matters are now judged by those with the power to judge: 1) it will allow for proper social distancing to avoid communicable diseases; 2) no more miserable commutes back and forth to work and the associated wasted resources and time such commuting causes not only for individuals but for society; 3) reducing the cost of doing business by transferring overhead costs over to employees without need of paying higher wages; 4) no more expensive commercial leases for office and business space or at least greatly reduced lease expenses for such space; 5) allowing for both home and work to be located almost anywhere instead of being forced into crowded cities and their urban problems, high cost of living, and associated misery and disease spread; 6) allow for a cleaner and better social and natural environment for all who are naturalized to it while also allowing for better control and management of any social outcastes; 7) no more having to deal in-person and personal with the miserable struggles for power between the Self and the Other.

When the Other is simply an image or a voice in a Searlean Chinese Room, it is simple and easy to resolve the conflict: you just close the screen or turn the computer off. If you do have an Other at your WFH, they will be roommates, significant others, spouses, or whoever you choose or reject and not those chosen by your employers without your input. In almost every technological material way, the reality of WFH and what is now considered artificial or virtual reality is pragmatically better than having to deal with the actual reality of personal and physical contact and especially the natural world. Eventually, VR and even the well-marketed AI will be considered and be used as meaning for "personal contact" in the same way the fictions of physics such as "atomic particles" and many other fictions in the sciences and the pseudo-sciences varying from "evolution" to the "sub-conscious" are now considered more real than the reality of what we actually experience. Already for most of the humanities, words such as the Self, the Other, Whiteness, and Blackness, are more real than any white or black person or any individual person or any particular state of affairs or experience actually perceived and experienced.

However, in my contemplations, I expected such a Room 101 reality to come to be in the same way reality is usually created in history: gradually over time or as the result of a natural catastrophe such as earthquakes or volcanoes or something similar. (But, not as a result of war. War is lawless. Because law in Technological Society has a monopoly on violence, any war that occurs would consist of legal acts of violence and thus not really be war just the rule of law exercising its power; the only acts of war that will occur will be individual acts of violence by fanatics who are outside of society and thus cannot socially construct social power.) Recent events have proven me wrong on this expectation. I greatly underestimated the power and the

Powers of Technological Society.

Within a matter of just the past few weeks, the Powers and their technicians of Technological Society have been able to construct socially a new world order consisting of a WFH Room 101 reality not only without a bang but even without a whimper. Sure, armed police and military are around to highlight this new world order, but they were and are not necessary. People have just marched into their new WFH Room 101 reality willingly, knowingly, and without complain like the banality of good expects of them — heck, even the bad people and the banality of evil have gone along with it. It is both amazing and scary to watch. As with much of Technological Society, its power is a much more impressive creation than anything the natural world has created or prior history has created — except of course for us. Natural creation requires a bang; Technological Society has now reached the point where like a god it creates naturally and by extension — both the Self and the Other become a virtual unity while the individual self and other individuals are still completely separate but irrelevant in reality. Diversity is maintained physically while completely eliminated where it matters. It is what all post-modern social justice theory both liberal and conservative has always wanted: an orderly and peaceful world under the rule of law in which any violence not naturalized to the rule of law is restricted to the spiritual purgatory or hell that may be the existential soul of the expendable individual and is thus irrelevant.

I will also say "I told you so" on the technique used for achieving this Brave New World: 1) by a random and arbitrary will to power of the Powers; 2) by the existential Heart of Darkness in all of us. I have gotten into greater detail on these two concepts in other writings (Existential Philosophy of Law and An Existential Meta-Ethics) but will summarize how they have been at work in the last few weeks.

The pragmatic work of finding treatments and cures for the recent Wuhan Virus as for any virus or for any problem requires pragmatic descriptions that can be used to solve such problems. However, as any nihilist should know by now, it is a complete waste of time to seek explanations for the normative classification of the Wuhan Virus as a pandemic or for the normative social actions taken, either voluntarily or forced upon society by governments, as a result of such classification. All non-existential knowledge is pragmatic: something is true and objective to the extent it solves a problem. As recently as the first week of March, there was no agreement among major health organizations including among the so-called experts at the World Health Organization as to how to define "pandemic" nor how to combat one if the definition is agreed upon and satisfied — there still is no agreement. These disagreements and their history are readily available on the internet. Calling something a pandemic, epidemic, or any such classification intended not to solve a problem but to create normative value for a problem is itself normative and is thus created recursively or based on implicit or explicit assumed axioms. Any such classification is not required foundationally by any premises argued as logically required by that classification. If you believe something to be a pandemic, you will find statistics to support your belief. If you believe something is not a pandemic, you will find statistics to support your belief. Your belief decides what statistics are relevant and material and not the other way around. Likewise, the normative determination of what actions to take in response to a pandemic are created arbitrarily and randomly by those with the power to make these determinations and are then justified by reference to statistics and not the other way around. For some forever unknown reason, the technicians and the Powers-that-be of Technology Society decided that this year they would call the Wuhan Virus a pandemic and decided the normative value of controlling its spread through government destruction of the world economy and of personal individual freedoms in the United States was of greater value than suffering deaths by the virus to avoid the deaths and other harms that would result from economic collapse and failure to protect those freedoms.

As a historical contemplation, it would be nice and fun to contemplate why Technological Society used this particular virus instead of some other problem to make its leap into the next stage of its historical development just like it would be nice to know why history led to the World Wars I and II and not some other world wars. However, as with any historical event, no one will ever know exactly why this-instead-of-that occurred and any answers will be pragmatically useless because history does not repeat itself. Always remember the nihilist motto: reality does not happen for a reason, it just happens.

What is most definitely existentially true and thus objectively true by the nature of our existential Heart of Darkness is that the pandemic classification and the normative actions taken were not altruist: the mass hysteria of the last few weeks was not done out of unselfish caring for the weak, elderly, sick, or the innocent children of the world or as a result of some kind of "innate goodness" in the Powers who control social construction. It is descriptively true based on historical experience that there will be an internationally spread flu or some other virus every year that will kill at least >600,000 people almost all of whom will consist of either the weak, elderly, sick, or innocent children. In 2019, on average 15,000 children under the age of 5 died every day as a result of malnutrition, under nutrition, or outright starvation — a figure that will most certainly go up this year as a result of global economic collapse. One guided solely by altruism could make a very rational argument that every day should have a pandemic declared and that all of world society should consist of being one big hospital entirely dedicated to taking care of the weak, elderly, sick, or innocent. Why the Powers randomly and arbitrarily decided to pick the Wuhan Virus to create temporarily such a world so as to change world culture is a mystery and will remain so but without doubt it resulted from a will to power not from altruism. The Outer Party government officials enforcing the Inner Party's will to power of Technological Society through forcing house imprisonment, unemployment, and loss of small businesses as a result of declaring a pandemic upon the world are doing so because they have nothing to lose and are not themselves suffering — for the moment and so they think. If the enforcers of a "pandemic" were themselves thrown into unemployment, economic loss, and imprisonment by the declaration of a "pandemic", it would never have been declared.

Unfortunately, the news is full of examples of this will to power at work. One of the most disgusting examples was given by New York Governor Andrew Cuomo. I am old enough to remember his father former Governor of New York Mario Cuomo whose political success I followed because he was expected at one point to become the first Italian-American presidential candidate and perhaps even first President. I am Italian by birth and Italian-American by social construct. Mario Cuomo always struck me as being a psychopath. Unlike the other Mario Cuomo son who works at CNN and who seems pretty much to be an idiot, this son Andrew is no idiot and seems to have followed in the psychopathic footsteps of his father as exhibited by his cold-blooded and hypocritical ability to justify based on Christian love his exercise of government power to violate every federal and state constitutional protection there is against tyrannical exercise of government power. Specifically, he chastised those who oppose his actions by preaching about his love for his 74, 84, or whatever year old (forgot how old she is) mother and his Christian sense of love and duty to protect all elderly and the defenseless weak, sick, and innocent children endangered by the Wuhan Virus. This dude like his father is supposedly a practicing Christian and a power in the New York Christian community who has no problem supporting infanticide in the form of abortion and signed new law authorizing abortion as late as the last trimester of a pregnancy — something his father had no problem doing also. So, yeah right, he respects the life of the elderly, weak, and sick because they are innocently helpless to defend themselves but has no problem with killing the ultimate defenseless and innocent life of a prenatal infant in order to help his political career.

Dudes like these controlling the pandemic classification and response would knowingly and intentionally kill any one of us if it would give them just a slight increase in godly power over us and are what made extermination camp management possible and efficient. They care nothing for saving life or for taking life unless it gives godly meaning to their own life. Unfortunately, they are common in the Christian community as its "leaders". No doubt, for example, the famed St. Augustine (a fricken Saint no less) and his ability after half-a-life of sinful debauchery to find his salvation in his faith that included justifying infant damnation was of the same psychopathic soul as this Cuomo family. Nietzsche would love their will to power as that of his Übermensch but I place their likes at the same level as that of psychopathic scum.

So, getting an explanation of the new world order in Technological Society is irrelevant. It happened for the same existential nihilist reasons everything happens in life: the random and arbitrary indeterminate nature of the universe and our existential Heart of Darkness. The big question is what now? For the wage slave poor now living life in the WFH Room 101 of Technological Society or out in the field serving these new school WFH slaves: must they also love this new life as victors submitting irreparably to technical slavery?

Why Does God Hate the Poor: Virus Supplemental Part II

The individual is in a dilemma: either he decides to safeguard his freedom of choice, chooses to use traditional, personal, moral, or empirical means, thereby entering into competition with a power against which there is no efficacious defense and before which he must suffer defeat; or he decides to accept technical necessity, in which case he will himself be the victor, but only by submitting irreparably to technical slavery. In effect he has no freedom of choice. — Ellul, Jacques. The Technological Society. Vintage Books: N.Y., N.Y. (1963) p. 84.

From a will to power perspective, the last few weeks of mass hysteria have been Technological Society ("TS") at its best and one of its finest works of art. Not just one nation's culture but the entirety of world culture has changed drastically and substantively without any bloating bodies strewn about the streets or blood running in the gutters — no armies and navies fighting, no extermination camps, no mass rallies of armed crowds roaming the streets, no cities covered in volcanic ash, no cities swallowed by earthquakes, and none of the other natural or historical events that usually are the foundation for cultural revolution. Complain about it all you want and call the Powers of TS names such as corporatism, capitalism, communism, neo-liberalism, socialism, or whatever, but the factual reality is that the Powers of TS ordered everyone to imprison and isolate themselves and everyone followed orders — cleanly, easily, antiseptically, and without any fuss or protest. In fact, any protest would seem monumentally evil because the orders get their validity based on the innocent deaths of some elderly and other sick who most likely would have died of something else instead of the virus anyway; since they would have died anyway, TS does not even need martyrs or human sacrifice to achieve cultural revolution. The Powers of the past must be rolling in their graves admiring the beauty of this exhibition of power for the sake of power.

Of course, the bodies and blood are still there. Just the higher suicide fatalities resulting from the forced isolation will most likely cancel out any lives saved by this pandemic cure. Even before the collapse of the world economy, on average 15,000 5-year-old and younger children died each day from malnutrition, under nutrition, or starvation; no doubt, these deaths will now go up by thousands more daily with global economic collapse. The educational system was barely educating the working classes as it was; now that they have lost a whole semester isolated at home while the upper classes afford on-line education and tutors for their children, I doubt they will ever catch up and will be permanently under-educated. The massive destruction and loss of life caused by the pandemic cures will far exceed the number of lives of the elderly and others it supposedly saved but this destruction and death will be hidden and not in the mass propaganda describing and explaining its history and thus they do not matter.

As always in TS, it is tough to make conceptual sense of what is going on because there is so much going on, no one knows what is going on, and no one knows what they are doing. Yet, not only does everyone go about pretending they know and talking about how much they know, but then from their tower of ignorance they pass judgment on the lives of others and decide what others ought to be doing as a matter of ultimate normative value — define the morality and ethics of the state of affairs. Most of the time it does not matter and is just yalking with no value other than perhaps as aesthetics in some form, but when those doing the yalking have the power actually to enforce their value judgments upon others, it does matter and it matters big time. At that big time moment, in just a few weeks, even without any natural catastrophe or war but peacefully through the monopoly on violence that is the rule of law, world culture arbitrarily and randomly changes drastically, substantively, and forever. This is the will to power freedom TS grants its gods.

What about the rest of us? Unless one is suicidal, as Ellul eloquently wrote, acceptance of TS is required because it is "a power against which there is no efficacious defense and before which [we] must suffer defeat". But, does the acceptance of technical slavery allow for any substantive freedom of choice for the will to power of the technical slave? How does the technical slave continue their will to power struggle and thus continue class struggle so history may continue?

In terms of being naturalized to reality, TS on the surface appears to deny the rest of us freedom of choice as we become bound to technical slavery. However, as I have argued elsewhere in more detail (Such as at Existential Meta-Ethics), the acceptance of material technical slavery in order to be a victor in life through the material prosperity it gives does not necessarily negate substantive freedom of choice for the human mind and the will to power of the individual soul. Technical slavery is not unnatural or an anomaly, it is the natural flow of history. This recent Wuhan Virus events and the associated mass hysteria further elucidate my arguments that nihilism allows for nihilist Acceptance: we can knowingly and intentionally accept our fate in life but without loving it and without making it our life's meaning in order to give meaning to our life and our lives. This new school freedom of choice is founded upon what was once old school theological agnosia; it is the freedom nihilism grants us even while physically imprisoned and most definitely while technically imprisoned by the will to power given to the Powers of TS by its godless Fates or even by God. This nihilist freedom of Acceptance is a freedom not even granted the Powers. Ultimately they need godly power over us and, if God is in fact the source of all authority, they need the God who grants this will to power so as to give meaning to their lives. We however do not need godly power over them nor any godly power over anyone including over ourselves to give meaning to our lives. Ultimately, the Powers need us but we do not need them. This is their one weakness that must be exploited so as to struggle and to overcome them and ourselves to defeat out technical slavery. This Acceptance gives nihilists the power not only to reject the Powers but also to reject God or to accept God: the ultimate freedom of choice and the ultimate godly power.

Pragmatically, we must first see that Acceptance of technical slavery in TS is not something that we should see as a weakness or as an existential bad faith surrender to lack of authenticity or whatever other phrases about which the some hypocritically pontificate to ignore their own status as technical slaves. As a matter of practical reality, in addition to being conceptually necessary, to be a victor in TS for anyone who is not one of its gods regardless if one is a simple proletariat or an intellectual proletariat requires one accept technical slavery. There were never any "good old days" nor any "noble savage" who had a greater freedom than anyone living in TS including any wage slave workers in TS. In the past, workers may have had a different kind of freedom but it was not any better. If one's hunter-gatherer tribe or ancient classical tribe became too tyrannical, for millennia workers including slaves — if smart and lucky enough — had the freedom to run away one day and to start another tribe in the next valley, hill, or wherever they could survive. This type of freedom however requires the knowledge of how to survive in reality as-it-is and does not allow for the freedom of creating reality as it ought to be. This old school freedom is missing in TS and gone forever. It is a different type of freedom but not any better or worse than we have now consisting of the freedom to decide how reality ought to be — to declare "God is dead" and pretend we mean it.

The last century or so of human history despite all its problems has been the most materially prosperous and peaceful time in human history in which while growing from one billion in 1900 to more than six billion population in 2000, workers have for the first time in human history enjoyed freedom from: chattel slavery; world famine; true plagues of truly pandemic proportions such small pox, polio, measles, the Black Death, the Antonine Plague, and many more deaths that lacked any cure or any concept of a cure; unsanitary water; unsanitary living conditions; world pestilence; locusts causing mass suffering; mass sufferings due to the vagaries of weather and nature; and much more. The freedom to change one's tribe at will simply by physically leaving one's social constructs allows one to look and admire the heavens from any place on earth but it cannot give one the power to actually discover, explore, and conquer the heavens. TS gives us freedom from material imprisonment so that we are free to confront the reality of imprisonment of the soul and its mind in this meaningless life if we have the courage to do so.

This confrontation is a necessary aspect of TS that cannot be eliminated because it flows naturally from the nature of its technique though it can be ignored if one lacks the courage to confront it. One can see this necessary aspect of its nature working in the simplest of techniques in which pragmatics provide a foundation for a will to power leap to creation of morality and ethics. For example, if one pragmatically needs a bridge for the purpose of carrying 5000 tons of vehicles, one does not engineer a bridge capable of carrying 5000 tons of vehicles. I am not sure what the engineering standards are these days, but most likely the technique for the technology of building a 5000-ton load bridge is to engineer at least a 10,000 ton load bridge and mostly likely a 40,000 or more ton load bridge depending on one's arbitrary and random choice of the morality and ethics of such risk decisions. Likewise, if with certain conjectures or assumptions, medical technicians build a modeling of the Wuhan Virus in which millions of persons die, this leaves open the option for calling it a pandemic and for the Powers of TS to use their power to define morality and ethics so as to force self-imprisonment and social isolation and so forth for all. Why would they do it for this model instead of for the 15,000 five-year-olds actually dying per day model or for any other modeling for problems that have equivalent or worse scenarios? Again, respective to the godly exercise of power as an end in itself, asking for such an explanation is a meaningless question and misses the point of godly power just as it does respectively for the power of God. God is power; the gods of TS are power. The gods of TS just as with God can do whatever they want when they want to do it — power is an end in itself. The fact they can arbitrarily and randomly exercise their power of creating morality and ethics purely as a will to power is a necessary aspect or attribute of their power; by definition, morality and ethics is in their power to define.

The spiritual questions of freedom of the soul and mind for meaning in life are the same in TS as they always have been. In fact, TS allows for the existence of the intellectual proletariat and their freedom — which is based not on knowledge but on ignorance and verbiage to hide ignorance — to work on these questions. The intellectual proletariat technical slaves appear to be above slavery because it is their technical task to sit in the stands and criticize the techniques of those slaves struggling in the blood and sand of the arena, but in the end they are just as expendable to TS as those struggling below. These questions of freedom in TS, instead of being expressed by shamans in religious or mystical expressions or even by the Platonic contemplations of philosophers as expressed in the past, are now expressed in popular media and aesthetics by post-modern shamans through aesthetically pleasing phrases that are in denial as to their equally religious, mystical, and Platonic nature: such phrases as authenticity, inauthenticity, angst, bad faith, despair, slave morality, master morality, the self, the other, self-identity, whiteness, blackness, and all the other post-modernist favorites complaining about the weaknesses of the "herd" as they like to call wage slaves among themselves as they look down on us from the stands while pretending to empathize with us. Again, the concepts are different but not any better nor worse. What there is now is the freedom to be purely aesthetic about these concepts and to ignore their pragmatics.

In prior cultures before TS, when exercising the freedom to leave and to create a new culture, one had actually to know how to physically survive; if one did not pragmatically know how to survive in reality, one did not survive reality. This was true as much of the tribal shaman as it was for the tribal hunters and gatherers; even the tribal shaman needed to know how to hunt, farm, gather food, and so forth and needed a record of success or the tribe would find another and the shaman would starve. Such is no longer true. The power of aesthetics in TS allows for survival independently of having any pragmatic knowledge of survival or of reality other than the ability aesthetically to create delusion more real than reality or to create what reality ought to be through fictions and verbiage. It no longer matters if our TS tribal shamans have any record of success or any record other than being able to convince through propaganda that they ought to have a record of success. Even failure can become a successful basis for power in TS if one controls the successful propaganda techniques available in TS.

If you look at how most of the proponents of the above aesthetically pleasing terms actually lived their lives instead of how they preach others ought live their lives, the practical reality of their necessary conceptual Acceptance of technical slavery in their own lives so as to have the freedom to complain about it is easily seen. If it is good enough for them, it is good enough for the rest of us to accept and to go on to the bigger questions of freedom of the will to power of the individual mind and soul. For example, even for Jacques Ellul, he had his chance explicitly to fight the last explicit imposition of technical slavery upon the world during World War II; he instead spent it making a good living as a potato farmer in Vichy France selling his product into the high demand created by TS and its World War II so he could survive to be critical of TS once liberated. Vichy France provided post-modernist hero Foucault with the formal education and the freedom to engage in his sexual escapades so that after liberation he could go on to complain about the West that liberated him and their supposedly destructive and oppressive power over the individual — though apparently he was not really seeking liberation nor needed liberation and could have continued living the life he wanted just as well under the tyranny of fascism or under the tyranny of communism as long as they left him alone to satisfy his sexual desires including sexual needs involving minors. The greats like Sartre, Beauvoir, and even my working class hero Camus and many more preachers of authenticity spent those World War II years — again, the last great opportunity for explicitly struggling against explicit technical slavery — enjoying the cafes of Paris and Marseilles and the critical adulation of both Vichy and German literary critics. These examples are countless. Intellectual proletarians are technical slaves as much as the rest of us but are simply in denial as to their status. Those who were or are not able to accept their technical slave status usually died fighting it either at the hands of others or by their own hand in physical or spiritual suicide.

Camus at least during his war years developed the idea of his book The Plague which is being rediscovered in this recent mass hysteria by the intellectual proletarians of the New York Times, the Washington Post, National Public Radio, and some others while completely ignoring — or not realizing — that the plague in The Plague was an allegory for fascism and Stalinist communism. They have also ignored the relevance to the recent mass hysteria of such books as Orwell's 1984 and Huxley's Brave New World. Most definitely, they have not rediscovered Friedrich Hayek's Road to Serfdom ("'Emergencies' have always been the pretext on which the safeguards of individual liberty have eroded.").

It is the success of TS in creating freedom from material imprisonment that is its most powerful technique for creating spiritual and mental imprisonment through technical slavery for those who either lack the courage to face this new school type of imprisonment or who enjoy their technical slavery as acceptable mental and spiritual meaning in life. One of the reasons the recent Wuhan Virus has resulted in mass hysteria is because a large proportion of the world population especially in the West has gone their whole life without ever experiencing death or unbearable physical or even deep tragic emotional pain or emotional isolation from society and most definitely without experiencing actual plague, pestilence, famine, war, or anything approaching catastrophic social collapse. This is good; as I have said before, given a choice between my child growing up in a world of violence in which by necessity only the strong and the fittest survive accustomed to the traumatic misery of life or of their growing up in a peaceful world in which all survive and the strongest must by choice work at being fit and strong to the traumatic misery of life, I will always prefer the latter peaceful option. In the latter, the pragmatic reality is that the weak as well as the strong will survive thus perhaps weakening the chances of survival for all and the chances of our exploring, discovering, and conquering the universe; but, since one never knows whether you or your children will be among the weak or the strong, if possible, my love for myself and for them would prefer the latter option. T.S. makes the latter option more practically possible, acceptable, and workable than in any prior time in history.

So, given that acceptance of technical slavery is necessary to be a victor in TS and thus in life, it is not something of which workers should be ashamed or be ridiculed as bad faith lack of authenticity or whatever ridicule elitists have of those who are not their gods. The important question is what freedom of choice does nihilist Acceptance of this new school slavery give to those who have the courage to confront the mental and spiritual aspects of this technical slavery? The answer is that there is a will to power freedom of mind and soul possible for the technical slave. It is founded on a new school nihilist version of the old school concept once know as theological agnosia from the philosophy of Pseudo-Dionysius or Dionysius the Areopagite: "unknowing" or agnosia is not ignorance or absence of knowledge as ordinarily understood but rather the knowledge that no language can express that which is beyond and above language. TS will always have gods who know what ought to have ultimate value and how others ought to live their lives. For the rest of us, the power of our will to power is to live without knowing either. The gods of TS will always convert their knowledge of good and evil into morality and ethics with its final attribute of violence. For the rest of us, the power of our will to power is to live without this knowledge and without this attribute.

Why Does God Hate the Poor: Virus Supplemental Part III

> *The individual is in a dilemma: either he decides to safeguard his freedom of choice, chooses to use traditional, personal, moral, or empirical means, thereby entering into competition with a power against which there is no efficacious defense and before which he must suffer defeat; or he decides to accept technical necessity, in which case he will himself be the victor, but only by submitting irreparably to technical slavery. In effect he has no freedom of choice.* — Ellul, Jacques. <u>The Technological Society</u>. Vintage Books: N.Y., N.Y. (1963) p. 84.

The new school epistemic agnosia of nihilism: the only certain or foundational knowledge you have is that you exist, you think, and want more than just existence. All else is unknowing, you know nothing else. These existential meanings are present in all words but precede the meanings of all words and thus are something of which in reality we cannot speak and of which we should be silent and thus are pragmatically meaningless. These existential meanings do serve as the implicit axioms or recursive meanings of all words and all language and of everything else pretending to be foundational knowledge. All such non-existential knowledge is uncertain at best and usually just made-up of socially constructed verbiage intended to hide there is no other foundational knowledge but only pragmatic knowledge and beliefs sometimes called truth for aesthetic effect and sometimes called normative or morality for the same aesthetic effect. At this point, you can accept what you are as you are and the world as it is: a slave can accept being a slave and make do, a king can just as easily and most likely even more easily accept being a king and make do, and so forth. This would be an optimistic nihilist. An existential nihilist would take the next step consisting of an act of will wanting more to life than just mere existence — a will to power. With this act of will, a slave would demand to be a king and a king would demand to be a god and all can demand love from a god or even from God, and so forth. It is this act of will that creates and leads to the struggle between the nihilist and existential reality which results in a life of absurdity and an existential choice that life either is worth living or is not worth living and what to do about that worth or lack thereof. As Orwell wrote in 1984, "[t]he choice for mankind lies between freedom and happiness and for the great bulk of mankind, happiness is better". In summary, all you really know is that you do not know; ultimately, freedom may be just an illusion anyway, so the choice of being a technical slave is as viable, sound, and valid as choosing not to be one.

The first freedom of choice allowed a technical slave if they want it:

choose to be one knowingly, intentionally, and holistically in the context of the indifference to the universe to your choice. Do not do it because it is the moral choice to make; because it is the ethical choice to make; because Divine Law requires it; because Natural Law requires it; because the law requires it; or for any other reason pretending your choice has ultimate normative value to anyone other than yourself. In the end, no one not even God cares, only you care — if you care. If the Room 101 prepared for you by Technological Society (TS) makes you happy and you want it, then live it and love it. Like Winston, look up and love Big Brother with a tear in your eye and be happy until the bullet enters your brain — it awaits all of us as would be made clear on this Easter Sunday by true believers if they were not too scared of Big Brother to go to church. If those who "truly" believe in a Resurrection can cowardly hide in the corner, the rest of us certainly can.

The second category of freedom allowed a technical slave if they want it: it is not to reject technical slavery because this is not allowed anyone in TS, but to hate it even to hate it with your whole heart, mind, and soul. You are a slave but that does not mean you have to like it and especially you do not have to love it. "To the end I grapple with thee; from Hell's heart I stab at thee; for hate's sake I spit my last breath at thee." You owe a duty to yourself to do what you have to do to survive as a slave if you want to survive and even to prosper as a slave if you want to prosper. You even have a legal duty to act as a slave so as to avoid going to jail. You even have an ethical duty to act as a slave because ethics is ruling class ideology and all present TS ruling class ideology requires you be a slave. However, you have no duty to be honest, skilled, happy, or anything "good" in your slavery; you have no moral duty, Divine Law duty; Natural Law duty; or any type of ultimate normative value duty to be a slave. You are one because you want to survive, prosper, and not go to jail. If something better comes along or you can get away with dishonesty, negligence, cheating, breaking the law, or anything in your duties as a slave, all without getting caught and punished by the Powers and gods of TS, then do it. In the end, it does not matter to anyone other than yourself. Even if there is a Resurrection, remember Christ died for all sinners as a criminal and outcaste Himself who only gave to Caesar the minimum the law required and no more, so you are still all set — except unlike Him hopefully you will be smart enough not to get caught. You have the ultimate freedom: to reject God or to accept God as He, She, or It is and not how They ought to be.

These two categories of freedom of choice and are the power that slaves have to continue class struggle and thus to continue history. They are not available to the Powers and gods of TS because their meaning in life is a purely self-served need for power: they must have a morality to force upon others; they must have an ethics to force upon others; they must have Divine

Law, Natural Law, and all the other laws to force upon others. If in fact all authority comes from God, then in addition to their socially constructed gods, rules, and laws, they must also have God despite their aesthetically pleasing protests of the opposite. They cannot think holistically because the world and the universe revolves around them and their self-served need for the power of gods or of God. This is their only weakness. Not much of one but slaves must take what they can get and run with it.

Some will object that such nihilist morality is really just anarchy that will result in another world of Nazi and Communist extermination camps and global political and economic collapse. This nonsense admits to both a lack of understanding as to the nature of TS and a delusion as to the Heart of Darkness that is the substance of our nature. If history repeats itself and the conditions are ripe for Governor Cuomo and the law or some other political pyschopath rule of law Inner and Outer Party Powers and gods to wake up one day and decide that extermination camps are needed to stop a virus pandemic in the same way their predecessor godly creators of moralities and ethics decided to stop what they considered to be a people pandemic, the reality is that what present moralities and ethics will do is the same as what Ellul, Sartre, Beauvoir, Foucault, and 95% of people did last time: nothing. Slaves do not control the Powers and gods of TS, they control us; there will always be morality and ethics in TS or in any society to control its slaves be they chattel, wage, or the slaves of technology. The extermination camps of the past will not occur because those techniques failed and were grossly inefficient. TS has morally and ethically grown beyond them.

Armed force is too efficient and dirty. Creating moralities and ethics that march people into self-imprisonment, self-isolation, and even self genocide (i.e., abortion for Blacks; wars in the Mideast for Christians; feminism for women) is much more efficient and the easier means to victory for the Powers and their gods. Again, do not forget the beauty of the last few weeks: not just one nation's culture but the entirety of world culture has changed drastically and substantively without any bloating bodies laying in the streets or blood running in the gutters — no armies and navies fighting, no extermination camps, no mass rallies of armed crowds roaming the streets, no cities covered in volcanic ash, no cities swallowed by earthquakes, and none of the other natural or historical events that usually are the foundation for such cultural revolution. This cultural revolution was accomplished even without martyrs or human sacrifice. (Well, without explicit martyrs and human sacrifice that make the headlines, so they do not matter.)

This finally leads me to the big question at issue in these multi-part essays: Why does God hate the poor? Why did God defined as the reason there is something instead of nothing create a reality with a necessary hierarchy? Why will there always be a small powerful ruling class (Powers, Outer Party, Inner Party, and so forth) who can positively control reality so as to create a world and gods in their image and then there will be the rest of us who are stuck only with the negative power to oppose whatever they are doing? Why must there always be a class struggle in order for history to continue and so we can go on to discover, explore, and conquer the universe?

Why Does God Hate the Poor: Virus Supplemental Part IV

> *The creation of Man whom God in His foreknowledge knew doomed to sin was the awful index of God's omnipotence. For it would have been a thing of trifling and contemptible ease for Perfection to create mere perfection. To do so would, to speak truth, be not creation but extension. Separateness is identity and the only way for God to create, truly create, man was to make him separate from God Himself, and to be separate from God is to be sinful. The creation of evil is therefore the index of God's glory and His power. That had to be so that the creation of good might be the index of Man's glory and power. But by God's help. By His help and in His wisdom.* — Robert Penn Warren. <u>All The King's Men</u> at pp. 658-59 (Houghton, Mifflin, Harcourt: N.Y., N.Y. 1996).

As stated in Part I of this series of supplemental essays, the last few weeks of mass hysteria have given me an opportunity to re-read Robert Penn Warren's *magnum opus* partly quoted above and to apply its conclusion and the mass hysteria to the original question of a previous longer series of essays in this blog: Why Does God Hate the Poor? Prologue / Part I? My original answer written several essays ago was:

> *He hates the poor because He can. He is the ultimate power and can do whatever He wants. In fact, since She acts by necessity, She must do whatever She wants. If you could choose your acts and had the power to do whatever you want, you would choose to exercise the power to do whatever you want. God acts by necessity, not from incompleteness requiring choice. He is what He is and can be.*

I then went on to ask and to decide if the answer matters or changes anything. My conclusion was that in the big scheme of things, it really does not. Why does God hate the Poor: Does the Answer matter? As a result of the last few weeks, have my conclusions changed any?

Warren's words are a true thing of beauty. In a few sentences, he has summarized libraries of theological verbiage. But, there are problems. The most relevant to the topic of this blog is that God may have created a God-less universe, but God most definitely did not create a god-less universe. Whatever help and wisdom She is granting creation, it appears to be limited or preferentially handed out only to the gods that make up a tiny portion of creation — by any measure they should be insignificant or at least of no greater power than anyone else but this is most certainly not the case. There is a hierarchy of help and wisdom resulting in a hierarchy of power that can be seen and described in words but not explained.

For the lifeless portion of the universe, be it made up of dark matter, dark energy, atomic particles that may or may not exist except when we observe them, numbers that are more real than the waves of nothing they describe, or whatever, in its benign inertness there is no "help" or "wisdom". The non-living universe spends its entire existence exploding so that it can then come back together to explode again — unless it just explodes back into the nothingness from which it came. It created life so that immediately after this creation it can begin trying to kill it and life can begin trying to survive. Is a virus alive or a form of life or is it just one of the countless things in the universe seeking to kill life? More likely, a "virus" is an example of how words are a form of life by giving order and meaning through social construction of language to the meaningless inertness that is the universe.

What about whatever we can agree upon as being life or alive? Does it have help and wisdom in some form?

Things are not much better for non-human life than it is for the universe. Considering a virus either to be or not to be life would not do much to change its existence just as it does not do much for other non-human life. For non-human life, it spends its entire existence not much better than the universe: explodes into life, hunts and kills each other for life, and then dies. Fortunately, non-human life does not appear to be self-conscious that this is their existence so they are free of the pain of this existential knowing.

How about human lives? Is there any help or wisdom there? The last few weeks like all historic events prove there is some help and wisdom available to human life if you are one of the few with the power to define "help" and "wisdom" so as to maximize the power of the few doing the defining. As with any words, "help" and "wisdom" are socially constructed relevant to the needs of a social group. The social construction of the meanings of these words is ultimately controlled by a small proportion — more accurately described as a handful — of individuals who have the power recursively to define "help" and "wisdom" or at best randomly and arbitrarily to define them axiomatically. Both definitions are done through their will to power and not based on any objective truth that exists independently of their will to power. God's help or wisdom is granted to a few and not to "Man" or to any significant portion of Man. Just as with everything from the first tribes on earth to the World Wars of the 20th Century and the pandemic of the last few weeks, a few decided what the rest of us ought to do and then we do it. If we do not like it, we used to be able to leave but even leaving is not allowed anymore. The gods speak about choice but that is all nonsense. For most of humanity, the choice is work or go to jail; in the last few weeks, for some the choice was stay home or go to jail. The will to power of these few gods not only defines what constitutes God's help and wisdom but goes on to create the aesthetics allowing them to pretend they are not acting as gods in a hierarchy of power but with the consent of those over whom they exercise their random and arbitrary godly power. The aesthetics consist of words such as: rule of law, social contract, will of the people, universal rights, social justice, and all the other social constructions aesthetically created to keep our Heart of Darkness in check so that the gods may rule.

Is that what all of this is about? A God-less creation means we are all "sinful" with this Heart of Darkness but it would be easy to forget this if we were all in fact gods with a power to create a world in our image. Maybe there are only a few gods so that only a few have the temptation to forget they are God-less. Is this the help and wisdom provided for most of us: to deny us a temptation we would most certainly not be able to resist and thus deny us failure?

I do not know the answer. In the end, I am stuck with agnosia but I do not like it and most definitely do not love it. I hate it. I must accept it to survive but hate it with my whole heart, mind, and soul. Given this agnosia and the act of will required to deal with it, the answer to my question does not really matter as at best it will be aesthetics as is Warren's answer. At that point, even the question does not matter. Asking the question pretty much answers it as it is a dead end.

It is this new school agnosia that is the biggest problem with the beauty of Warren's above epigram: the beauty created by Warren through the use and usefulness of words hides the ugliness of not knowing. As with all aesthetics, it is tempting to believe the words have something to do with a reality beyond the will to power of Warren or of any writer or other master of aesthetics but nihilists must resist this temptation. There is no "Man", "creation", "life", "beauty", "good", "evil", or any other words that can be used to ask my question or to answer it in reality other than in the reality of words. We created words, not God. There are six billion or so individual conscious lives on earth but there is no thing that is "life" on earth. For each, actual reality comes into existence when each individual soul becomes conscious of their existence and ceases when their consciousness ceases. Objective reality and truth may in fact exist before or after their consciousness and before and after my consciousness but it does not matter to the individual who is not around to be conscious of it; they also do not matter in a world of new school Technological Society agnosia lacking any non-pragmatic meaning for truth and most definitely lacking any for objective truth. Of objective reality and truth, all I know is nothing — not "nothingness" but actually nothing. There are six billion answers to my question — more accurately, there are six billion questions with six billion different answers. The answer to my question and even the question does not matter because both are an act of will by each of those six billion and not an act of reason. Whether one makes a leap to faith in the "glory and power of God" or a leap to the rejection of that faith, it is all a will to power leap to meaning in life as random and arbitrary as is life. Reason is a tool for making that leap work but it can give no reason for justifying any such leaps nor even for questioning them or answering any questioning of them.

Charity Not Love

The word 'love' is everywhere these days. From the actual and seriously taken presidential campaign of Marianne Williamson to all popular secular and religious philosophies. (Personally, I loved Williamson's campaign — for great comic relief if for nothing else. She seem to be the only real person in the whole bunch.) Love is seen as the answer to all problems involving human relations in almost any form. So, why is not "love" listed in any of the classical virtues going back to Plato's Republic nor in the list of Western theological virtues? These two sets of virtues total seven and consist of prudence, justice, temperance, courage (or fortitude), faith, hope, and charity. It is with good reason love is excluded and I am getting tried of hearing about love as if it is a cure-all. When everyone seems to agree on a concept, one should immediately be suspicious of it as either a delusion or a con.

As I contemplated in my essay asking Why Does God Hate the Poor: Can God Love? Part III , love is a self-centered act and one side of a two sided coin in which hate is the other side. One cannot know love if one does not know hate and the reverse. Love is the relationship we have to that which gives meaning to our life; hate is the relationship we have to that which denies meaning to our life. Love is the answer? To what? What is the question? So, love of money, power, sex, rape, child molestation, your tribe, or the almost uncountable number of acts most people would call evil and which the evil love are answers to evil? If you love your neighbor must you not hate if not the evil person who hurts them but the evil acts that hurt them? Must you not hate evil acts? According to those who preach love is the answer, you must hate and punish racism, sexism, fascism, and much more in order to be a truly loving person. Love is not the answer but only an answer to certain specific problems. Even assuming it is somehow possible to love your enemies, loving their evil acts only helps your enemies do evil to you and to others and to spread their evil acts — however you define evil. By definition, to love truly, you must hate the evil acts of those you love to help them see the Good.

As is often true, the Ancients and the Medieval Scholastics were wiser than much of modern philosophy in their contemplations and so they intelligently left "love" out of their list of virtues to instead include Charity. Charity is considered a theological virtue because supposedly it cannot occur naturally, it is a gift from God in which a person sees God and other persons not as a means to an end — such as achieving meaning in one's life — but simply as an end-in-itself. It is not a two-sided coin as is love and hate. Its absence is not uncharity or the state of being uncharitable but is simply its negation or absence — just as nothingness does not replace being as an state of existence but is simply nothing regardless of what Husserl, Heidegger, Sartre, or their worshipers otherwise preach in their aesthetics.

Is Charity a meaningful concept existentially or in any pragmatic form or is it itself simply aesthetics? Is it used and useful only in the same way as the words "Pegasus", "the Self", "the Other", or any of the other uncountable amount of words available for preachers of certain ethics and moralities to use to promote their self-centered images of how the world ought to be? Does it have pragmatic value for nihilism? Maybe. At a minimum, it gives us a word to use and is useful for pointing out the absurdity and the shallowness of the omnipresence of "love" in present society as another false god. Nihilists can do better than love.

Sympathia (Empathy: A Modern Socratic Dialogue)

CRITO: You have arrived at a very opportune moment Socrates. I was afraid you would be late.

SOCRATES: Has the festival started early?

C: No, there is plenty of time before it starts. I was worried you would miss an argument between Anytos and Phaidros regarding something closer to your heart, virtue. They were just about to end it, in order to avoid further antagonism, when I saw you were coming.

S: I hope I have arrived before the ending of the discussion, for I will learn from any discussion related to virtue, and after the ending of any anger that might have arisen.

C: I am sure they will be able to manage their differences and maintain a clear mind so that you can enter the discussion. It is a subject I want very much to hear your thoughts on, Socrates. Therefore, I ask them as a friend to explain the matter to you and I will listen and learn.

S: If it pleases them, I would willingly enter the discussion; not as a teacher, though, but as a student, one who has much to learn.

PHAIDROS: It is a simple matter. The discussion has been unnecessarily prolonged because of pride, on the part of Anytos

ANYTOS: Pride, perhaps, but it is not only on my part.

C: It seems I must lay the foundation for the renewal of the discussion. Phaidros has accused Anytos of practicing virtue to such an extreme that it has become an evil.

A: As if such a thing were possible; being virtuous has no limits.

P: My statements have been carried further than I intended. I have no hesitations about defending what I know to be true. I do not intend, though, to get entangled in abstract arguments involving the nature of virtue. To argue on such matters requires a special type of knowledge; one I do not really need for it would keep my head in the clouds much of the time. I am a practical man; I know the simple truths of life. Our argument involved a specific instance in which Anytos' empathic nature caused me a misfortune.

S: The nature of a virtue is a difficult topic. I have found, though, that there is no need to go too far from practical manners and simple ideas in order to find great difficulties. Since you do not have this problem, surely you will not deny me the chance to learn from you. If the matter is as clear and simple as you say, will not the knowledge you give me be also clear and simple?

P: I will make it as clear for you as I can.

A: Go on, tell Socrates the source of our disagreement.

P: A mutual friend of Anytos and mine owned me a monetary debt. Because he was suffering continuous misfortune, both personal and business, I was always anxious to have him repay it. Anytos, letting empathy rule him, advised me to give the man more time. The man left on a trading voyage some time ago and did not return at the designated time; nor will he ever return and neither will the payment of his debt.

S: Is empathy the virtue you claim Anytos has practiced blindly, without a consideration of practicality?

P: Empathy is only a virtue among women. It is a weakness among men. This instance clearly proves me right; it was empathy that made both of us look like fools.

S: When a physician fails to aid a sick man because he was called too late, the sick man was already dead or neat death, should the art of medicine be blamed?

P: No, it is the man's fault or his friends for failing to summon the physician earlier.

S: When an animal trainer is called upon to train an old animal whose habits are already set, if he fails, should the art of animal training be blamed?

P: No, the animal is un-trainable.

S: If justice is served upon a criminal, but the man fails to reform his life, is justice at fault?

P: Of course not.

S: If empathy is used when dealing with an ignorant soul and it fails to

96

achieve good results, would it be proper to blame empathy?

P: Perhaps I did make a hasty generalization. If we look at any acts of empathy, though, its consequences are always the same; it weakens the character of the man using it and leads to misfortune.

S: Before you assist someone in a search do you usually ask them what they are looking for?

P: Of course.

S: Before I look for acts of empathy with you to judge, I need to know what you define empathy to be.

P: Empathy is similar to pity. It is an act of the spirited part of the soul by which a person feels sorrow for an other's troubles.

S: Are not brothers similar in many ways yet never the same person?

P: Of course not, they are two different people.

S: Galleys and trading ships are similar yet also very different, are they not?

P: They are different.

S: Then pity and empathy, though they are similar, could also be very different from each other.

P: Yes, but I think the difference is very small.

S: Is it harmful for a ruler to pity his people?

P: Yes. The ruler is harmed because he is letting himself be affected by his emotions instead of being guided by reason. The people are being harmed because they are seen as inferior, as unable to overcome their troubles without aid of the ruler. The citizens will look badly on the ruler for having this opinion of them and will try to take advantage of his pity for their own purposes. Chaos will result.

S: Should a general pity his troops?

P: No, for the same reasons.

S: Should pity exist among friends?

P: No.

S: Has it not been written, though, by many leaders and wise men, that a good general should have empathy for his troops, a good ruler for the citizens, and that empathy should exist between friends?

P: Yes, I have heard that said many times.

S: Then perhaps we should search more diligently for the difference between pity and empathy.

P: If you think the search will not run into the drama.

S: Did you say that pity was an act of the spirited part of the soul?

P: Yes.

S: Is that also true of foolhardiness; is it not an act of the spirited part of the soul by which the soul endangers its mortal life for unnecessary and meaningless causes?

P: Yes, that is true.

S: What happens when this spirited act becomes governed by reason?

P: I don't understand.

S: If reason where to govern this spirited act, than there will be an understanding involved. Reason would enable the soul to understand what ideas are meaningful and necessary and worth risking one's life for; would not foolhardiness then become courage?

P: Now I understand; yes, that would be the difference between foolhardiness and courage.

S: Is this true for any act of the spirited part? If reason is allowed to govern it than it is no longer a weakness but a virtue.

P: I agree.

S: If pity were to be governed by reason, what new nature would be created?

P: I am not sure.

S: An understanding would surely be added, for we agreed to that. In the case of pity, would this be an understanding of an other's troubles and the feelings caused by these troubles, whether sorrow or cheering up is needed?

P: Yes, reason would add such an understanding.

S: Would this understanding be advantageous to a general for him to judge the morale of his troops, to a king for him to judge the mood of the citizens, and among friends so they may cheer one another up?

P: Yes, it certainly would be.

S: Could this understanding be the empathy spoken about and written about by so many men? Could this be the difference between the similar natures of pity and empathy?

P: It seems you have found it.

C: It is a very important difference. Such an understanding would greatly improve the social relations between men. I am glad you arrived in time to enter the discussion, Socrates.

S: Now we must go on to complete it.

A: What do you mean?

S: Now that we understand the nature of empathy, we must examine the original situation which created the need of defining it to see if it applies. Then, should we not go on to study if it is possible to practice it to an extreme?

P: Perhaps some other time, the drama is about to start.

A: I will look forward to it.

C: So will I.

S: So should we all, for we are all still students with much to learn.

The Truth on SJC Case 12025 / *In re* Valeriano Diviacchi

Private citizen Valeriano Diviacchi pursuant to the First Amendment states the following regarding SJC Case 12025, *In Re Valeriano Diviacchi* in which the undersigned Valeriano Diviacchi was the only attorney who had the courage to speak honestly and truthfully to the best of his knowledge and ability; who was the only attorney willing to handle a complex, difficult case on an honest and reasonable fee basis; who was willing to do so despite being out-of-state attending his daughter's college graduation at most material times (something no judge or BBO member could be bothered to consider nor even to mention); who represented his client in such a competent and diligent manner that his client avoided default, foreclosure, and true bankruptcy that would have been the undisputed result without his representation; and who committed no act of perjury nor intentional misrepresentation as falsely claimed in this case unlike the other attorneys involved who used his honest work and the deceptions of his client to collect their dishonest fees and to falsely disparage his work and experience to benefit themselves.

Private citizen Valeriano Diviacchi pursuant to the First Amendment states the following to the following specific individuals and generally to the American system of Injustice.

— To the "moral busybodies" of the Supreme Judicial Court who through appointment by a few, absolute immunity for their decisions, and life tenure have become a modern House of Stuart Star Chamber so accustomed to stating fact and "law" as necessary to enforce their own personal ruling class ideology that they have become incapable of differentiating fact from fiction and whose fear of losing their power prevents them from dealing honestly with the miserable lives who have the misfortune of appearing before them (remember the words of Upton Sinclair, "judges are not bought, they are selected");

— To the glorified bookkeepers that call themselves Bar Counsel and Board of Bar "Overseers" consistent with their plantation heritage and mentality whose only knowledge of ethics is how to spell it and including but limited to the hypocritical, delusional, sycophant, bigots who were involved in the above case who were and are willing to have their personal emotional dislike and professional jealousy of an individual they consider beneath their class serve as a basis for financial, personal, and familial punishment of that individual;

— To the fine, upstanding members of the post-modern cult called "the Bar" everywhere whose ignorance of history, the cowardice of the many, and the power of the few with the ability to contort ruling class rules of etiquette and self-interest into a recognizable and enforceable ethical standard makes them willing to destroy lives both physically and spiritually;

— And last by not least to my former client Camilla Warrender;

I state:

I did nothing morally wrong in this case other than to naively expect honesty and forthrightness from my client, the Bar, and the justice system. A mistake no honest trial attorney should make or they will wind up as I have in this case in which the published facts have little if any relation to what actually happened. Remember the words of C.S.Lewis:

"Of all tyrannies, a tyranny sincerely exercised for the good of its victims may be the most oppressive. It would be better to live under robber barons than under omnipotent moral busybodies. The robber baron's cruelty may sometimes sleep, his cupidity may at some point be satiated; but those who torment us for our own good will torment us without end for they do so with the approval of their own conscience." — Lewis, C. S. "The Humanitarian Theory of Punishment." *Issues in Religion and Psychotherapy*: Vol. 13 : No. 1 , Article 11 (1987) p. 151. Available at: https://scholarsarchive.byu.edu/irp/vol13/iss1/11.

Made in the USA
Middletown, DE
06 March 2021

34653448R00060